Eat Your Way to God

DISCOVER THE TREE OF LIFE!

Guy Caskey

Eat Your Way to God
Copyright © 2015 Guy Caskey, Houston, Texas

All rights reserved. No part of this publication may be reproduced, stored in a retrieval system, or transmitted in any form or by any means—electronic, mechanical, photocopying, recording, or otherwise—without the prior written permission of the publisher and copyright owner. The only exception is brief quotations in printed reviews.

Worldwide Publishing Group
Your multi-platform publishing partner
7710-T Cherry Park Drive, Suite 224, Houston, Texas 77095
www.WorldwidePublishingGroup.com
(713) 766-4272

The views expressed in this book are the authors and do not necessarily reflect those of the publisher.

Published in the United States of America

eBook: 978-1-312-87960-7

Softcover: 978-1542514576

Hardcover: 978-1-312-87959-1

What Others Say About This Book

"You will be blessed by the parallels of our physical function and how we function as a body of Christ. A healthier you is a more effective follower of Christ!"
- **Dr. Mick Mahan**, *Discover Chiropractic Health Center*

"The power that emanates from the pages of this book is the incredible congruity between the man and the message. Having been in his home many times I can tell you this material is not a theoretical postulation of truth for him, but a lifestyle that has borne fruit for many."
- **Mark Lecrone**, *Kingdom Professional, Philosopher, Pastor, Prophet, Elder*

"What an encouragement this book is to get back to living the way that our Father intended all along! Our nation is in real trouble, but there is still time to turn it around. Whether we're a parent, a grandparent, wife, husband or mentor, family meals and deep communication need to be part of our lives on a **regular** basis."
- **Peggi Merkey**, founder of *Can You Hear Me Now*, Evangelist and passionate youth advocate

"Guy Caskey has been catalyst in my life to not only share the gospel with the multitudes, but to take on the responsibility to disciple them. Prior to my relationship with Guy, my focus was primarily evangelism. Now that I am a part of the growing M4 Network, I have a much greater call and a strategic focus on how to train disciples to train disciples. I believe both our physical and spiritual health coincide in this book therefore making us more effective Christ-followers."

- **Bobby Tre9 Herring**, Christian rapper, Founder of *Eyes on Me, Inc.*, urban missionary, evangelist, and apostle.

Table of Contents

What Others Say About This Book 3
Introduction 7
Chapter 1 The Family Table What does your dinner say about you?......... 11
Chapter 2 Jesus and the Divine Dinner... 23
Chapter 3 Hospitality By Guy and Kelli Caskey 37
Chapter 4 Metabolize 53
Chapter 5 Fasting and Feasting.. 63
Chapter 6 Organic living: Living by Design (Physical Body) 75
Chapter 7 Organic Living: Living by Design (Soul and Spirit) 81
Chapter 8 The Environment Matters.. 103
Chapter 9 The Blights (Dis-eases) of Organic Life 113
Chapter 10 Organic Mission The Vision, the Mission and the Expression 125

Introduction

I have heard it said that the only way to eat an elephant is one bite at a time. This is certainly true when it comes to handling many of the complex issues of life; and nothing is more difficult than, or as complex as transforming cultures. The answers are often simple but also counterintuitive. How we eat is connected to how we live.

In America, we have lost our way. We don't put food in its rightful place – the way we eat is unhealthy and the rituals we associate with our food, which should be significant in our lives, are woefully missing. These patterns should serve as indicators that we are lacking the health and wholeness that we were designed for.

Have you ever ignored a check engine light or the temperature gauge on your car and ended up broken down on the side of the road? How about the times you've ignored a wilted plant until it was too late, and no amount of water could bring it back to life.

The way we are eating as individuals, as families and as communities is screaming out that we have a problem. Many of us are like broken down cars on the side of the road, or wilting and dying plants as a result. We no longer take the time to engage with each other in the depth of relationships God has designed us for over our meals. Our lack of focus on relationships, and our failure to meaningfully engage our spiritual and biological families at the dinner table is creating a vacuum of physical, spiritual, and relational health. It often seems that we are living to eat rather than eating to live. Our families rarely take the time to sit down and enjoy one another.

We are not sharing the crucial conversations about our lives with one another, or talking about God in a way that nourishes our hungry souls. We are slowly perishing by means of a fork and choosing the road most traveled as prescribed by our culture rather than by the Kingdom of Jesus Christ.

Here is "the skinny" on the situation: We are Fat! Americans have generally fallen out of shape physically, emotionally, relationally, and spiritually (body, soul and spirit). Like the proverbial "frog in the kettle," this has happened incrementally. Abnormal living has become our norm. When I use the word "fat" here, I am referring to an unhealthy way of life. You can actually be considered fat and still be rather fit; particularly, if you use a BMI chart. (Body Mass Index) That being said, the truth is--we CAN change! We can embrace patterns of health that can bring positive change to us as individuals, families, and communities. Imagine your life as a picture of health body, soul and spirit.

What would that look like?
What kind of changes would need to be made?
How do you make those changes?
What kind of environment is needed for these changes?

Many of us would say that we've tried, but failed. However, it's important that we know that it's not in trying, but in trusting, that we'll find that our strength is made perfect in weakness. But trusting involves training. (John 15; Hebrews 12:11)

Most of us want to be healthy, and there is hope for each of us. I've seen the difference that sharing meals and sharing life together can make. It's helped me connect to my Creator and Sustainer. If we are to be truly healthy, there are habits and principles for holistic health that we must follow. While it is true that there is hope, we aren't naïve enough to think we can reach perfection on this side of eternity. Our hope must blend with the reality that there are longings, and things in life beyond our comprehension, on this sin cursed planet.

There are times when things break down. There are times when we must face disease, and tragedy in this fallen world. That's why I love the resurrection power of Christ that provides hope right now, in good times or in bad--hope in Him for every season.

I love this quote from Tina Francis that reminds me of hope for today and a promise for the future:

> *"I dream of a table where no one feels excluded, uncivilized or ignorant. Where everyone is free to talk and eat to their heart's content. I dream of a place where every voice, age, sex, accent and story matters. Where cutlery and rhetoric are details; where every dinner roll and tongue is buttered with love. Where people revel as they touch, taste, inhale and savor the decadent goodness of God's love. With bare hands, bare feet and bare hearts."*[1]

There is a deeper story and a deeper way of life that we can live with Christ, and one another. So if the life we live around our food (the dinner table) really is that big of a deal, then what do we need to do?

The answer is simple, but not easy. Let's get back to the dinner table by having divine dinners. Have you ever observed how often a meal or gathering around the dinner table can deeply connect us with meaning and life-change? Have you ever observed the life of Jesus Christ and His followers?

Let me encourage you to take the Gospels of the Holy Bible: *Matthew, Mark, Luke* and *John* and read them and take note of how many illustrations of, and conversations around food are found in Jesus' teaching about God's Kingdom. We can experience God in powerful ways around the dinner table if we will open up our eyes and our lives.

In this book I will share with you what I have learned, am unlearning, not as some theorist, but as someone who has been practicing the very things I am about to share with you. Many have searched for the Tree of Life, but I have found it-- and it is truly life changing! It is an organic way of living with spiritual and relational vitality; connected to our Creator, fully functioning by design.

> "Then Jesus declared, "I am the bread of life. He who comes to me will never go hungry, and he who believes in me will never be thirsty" (John 6:35, NIV).

> "I am the true vine, and my Father is the gardener...I am the vine; you are the branches" (John 15:1,5, NIV).

Chapter 1
The Family Table
What does your dinner say about you?
Revelation 3:20-22

"Here I am! I stand at the door and knock. If you hear my voice and open the door, I will come in and eat with you, and you will eat with me. Those who win the victory will sit with me on my throne in the same way that I won the victory and sat down with my Father on his throne. Everyone who has ears should listen to what the Spirit says to the churches" (Revelation 3:20-21, NCV).

As I reflect on my childhood, I remember a few divine moments that I experienced with my family. To me a divine moment is something that sticks with me. It strikes a deep chord within my soul that creates a longing to connect with God and others.

Some divine moments are like the Morpheus quote in the *Matrix:* "Like a splinter in your mind."[ii] They create a longing for something that is missing. You may not quite know what it is, but you know something isn't right. You know that there must be more to this life. Hopefully, you have had that moment in your life when the God shape gap shared by us all is filled by the Author of Life Himself. Then you will know you are loved and can live a life that fully functions by design. If this is not real in your experience, my prayer for you is that you would hunger for more, and be filled.

The family, into which I was born, like most families, had its share of dysfunctions, difficulties, and disillusionments. At times it felt like a living hell, but I do remember some sweet moments; even before God invaded and plundered my life (in a good way, by the way). I remember Sunday mornings where I think I experienced something more like the church family Jesus intends for us to experience than what we have made "church" to be in many places around the globe today.

I remembered the thrill of my family gathering together, eating pancakes and listening to *American Top 40* with Casey Kasem[iii], and waiting with anticipation for the NFL's Dallas Cowboys football game to come on TV. There was something about those simple times that deeply connected with me, and with a longing to be satisfied to the core of my being (Maybe it was Aunt Jemima pancakes and syrup. Or was it the fact that I was hopped up on sugar?)

Oddly perhaps, I believe it was the mysterious longing to share a meal with Christ and His family, and to enjoy a spiritually intimate relationship with Him. In fact, I believe He shares a similar longing. For He says: *"Here I am! I stand at the door and knock. If anyone hears my voice and opens the door, I will come in and eat with him, and he with me"* (Revelation 3:20, NIV).

I am truly grateful for those times around the dining table with my family and of course I would be amiss if I didn't mention that there were certainly times where it was more like a holy war at the table than a divine moment. I have learned and observed that family conflict, in both biological and spiritual families, can help us become bitter or better.

As a young boy my dad was my hero and idol. But in time, I discovered that my golden idol, like all men had feet of clay. I admit that I felt pretty letdown by that experience, and by the expectations I had placed on dad. However, it was that letdown that led me on a journey that ultimately brought great healing as I discovered that there is a perfect Heavenly Father whose golden rule of love never fails. This has brought strength to my life as I came face to face with my own sin, idealism, and faulty expectations.

I have experienced God's cleansing forgiveness, and like Jesus, "I know who I am, and where I am going." My connection with God through Jesus Christ has strengthened me. Therefore, as all who walk in Christ-like maturity should, I endeavor to do the right things, for the right reasons, no matter the results. Today, my earthly father and I have a healthier relationship, filled with a great deal of love and mutual respect.

One of the things I have noticed in my family, and in other families with whom I have worked with as a minister of Christ, and mentor of others for over 20 years, is that when the dinner table is not a place of community, connection, and communication in a family, the family is weak and generally ineffective in accomplishing its divine purpose.

The divine purpose of a family is to be on mission with God reflecting His love and life, thus expressing it, to others through the family unit. This is also the purpose of Christ's body, the family of God "the church." And of course, there are those who are fortunate enough to have their biological family and spiritual family as one and the same.

The apostolic movement that was set forth by its founder Jesus Christ in the New Testament was based upon households of faith. (Luke 10; John 4:53; Acts 11:14, 16:31, 18:8; Romans 16:5, 10-11; 1 Corinthians 16:15; Ephesians 2:19-20; 1 Timothy 3:12-15)

One of the most revealing activities, in relation to families, that I have ever done is something I have been doing for years. I do it with adults and students. I call it *family table drawings*, and here is how it works:

This will require a piece of white paper, a white paper plate, or some construction paper; and some crayons, or map pencils, or colored fine point felt tip markers. Draw your family table: the place where you ate as a family the most when you were growing up. For many, this is can be a difficult and painful experience; but ultimately, when we are honest and desire God's help, it will be healing and insightful.

I like to illustrate my view of my family, as I saw it, when I was a teenager. I draw icon's representing each member as I remember them. For example, I will draw my father as a strong arm with a bulging bicep in bold black outline – he was strong, a provider, and a man's man. As a young boy I both feared and idolized him.

I would depict my mom as a red heart, with a glue residue around the edges. You see, I felt it was her love that held us all together.

My brother would be a button because he was the middle child and the ultimate button pusher. I often use the color brown for him.

I'd illustrate my sister as an egg with pig tails, and a yellow tiara. I thought she was the spoiled youngest child. Me? I would be a big black and blue head. Why? I did so because I was pretty full of myself, and very selfish.

I would then draw different lines of communication between one member and another member of the family. Some of the lines were like lightning bolts signifying them striking at each other. Other lines would be black broken dash lines representing on again, off again communication. I have even used arrows through a heart to represent lines of loving communication. All of this drawn around the rectangle Formica table my dad built where we had our aforementioned divine Aunt Jemima moments at the dinner table.

As good as some of those moments were, I used my *family table drawings* to describe how my parents had me as teenagers, and the relational difficulties they experienced. Some of those were perhaps because at times it seemed like dad was married to his job, and mom was married to us kids. Needless to say, we did not have the healthiest marriage modeled for us as we were growing up. Of course, today I realize that my parents did the best they knew to do with what they were given. For that I am very grateful.

One thing that has always gripped me about the *family table drawing* activity is the level of pain and dysfunction that can be traced back to our family of origin. Of course there are those who come from incredible families; some, whose parents prepared them for successful futures. While it is certainly true that our families do have a significant impact on our lives; the good news is that no matter what our family background, God can bring the necessary changes in our lives so we can overcome.

If our family was a mess it is not an excuse for poor behavior. A commitment to blame is a commitment to stay the same and never change! Admitting and understanding our dysfunctions can help us to identify some self-defeating root causes that are keeping us from being who God created us to be. God desires that all of His people express His life individually, and in communities (local bodies of Christ). He wants us to bear fruit abundantly, fruit that lasts. (John 15)

We need to figure out what this fruit is and how it is produced, and then reproduced. I don't believe this abundant fruit is health and wealth (by the way), although those could very well be secondary things gained as we seek first His Kingdom. The good news is that Christ promises to produce abundant fruit through us if we will trust Him. So we must remove, or prune, our distrust so that trust can produce His fruit through us.

We simply can't figure this out as long as we're living in the past, wallowing in the mire of our family's dysfunction. So be prepared. This process can and will surface some pretty negative things that we have come to embrace in our culture as normal and unfortunately it is.

When people create their *family table drawing*, some draw a house with everyone eating in separate rooms with no communication. Others draw people eating dinner around the TV set, with TV trays, chowing on TV dinners – notice the TV is mentioned a lot here? You can also imagine the honest answer of many who eat more often in the car than they do around a dinner table, killing themselves with fast food.

Just a side note, if you are single you probably eat a lot in the car. I encourage you to join a family and share a meal with them at least once a week! Before I was married, while still in my twenties, there were several families in my spiritual family with whom I shared meals. They helped me see and appreciate the significance of sharing meals together as a family. Most importantly, I came to realize that there was something being shared around the table that was so much more than a meal.

When families gather for a meal and really share their lives, it re-enforces the covenant that they have with God and one another. There is a mysterious commitment and connection that says: "When we share food, we share life--body, soul and spirit."

Here are a few suggestions you may wish to initiate around your dinner table.

At every meal at dinner time pray, and then allow each person a chance to share uninterrupted. Observe the Lord's Supper as a family from time to time as a symbol of communing or connecting with God and one another. We will talk more about this later. Make dinner a sacred time for sharing life together. Expect everyone to be there and everyone will serve each other as a team--a family unit. If your schedule does not permit this, then set aside time for family meals over the weekend. You could even do this at certain restaurants. The key is to spend time sharing life with each other. You may be less structured, which is great as long as you are intentional about engaging in conversations that allow each one to express him or herself.

As you make new transitions, be aware that it could be and most likely will be a bit chaotic and difficult at first. But in time the family will grow to embrace it. Remember, children will adjust to and conform to these changes if you stay consistent and stick to the process. Our son, who we adopted from Ethiopia when he was younger, had a very difficult time communicating his thoughts and feelings at first. But now there are times where he needs to be reined in a little after some time at the Caskey's dinner table.

If you know someone who is effectively experiencing shared life around the dinner table then see if you can arrange a time to join them and learn from them. I believe with all my heart that God can turn your empty banquet table into a celebration with divine wine. "Divine" comes from Christ, who called Himself the Vine, who brings forth life in the

Spirit, in us. In time, you should be able to invite others to join you and taste and see that the Lord is good.

It is true that the sins of our fathers are handed down from generation to generation, but that does not mean we have to commit those same sins, or that there is no hope. In Deuteronomy, God communicates to His people the impact sin's consequences have upon families, people groups and cultures. He says that when a family chooses to walk in sin, the fathers will reproduce consequences that will be handed down to the third and fourth generation.

Some today refer to this phenomenon as "family of origin issues." The sins of our family of origin are destructive behavior patterns that can actually impact entire cultures. The good news is that through Jesus Christ, and the multiplication of disciples, these generational curses can be reversed and cultures can be.

Jesus told his original disciples in Acts 1:8 to receive His power and multiply His life from Jerusalem, Judea, and Samaria to the ends of the Earth. He described a transformation movement accomplished by multiplying disciples to the ends of the earth. His was a big vision to think that by multiplying His life through a few, He could reach the world. I like to say in our trainings that "He had a big enough vision to think small."

Paul follows this pattern of change in 2 Timothy 2:2 by telling His spiritual son, Timothy, to invest his life in faithful men who will in turn invest in others. We have four generations of disciples (Paul, Timothy, faithful ones, and others). This indicates a movement and the beginnings of the kind of transformation that changes cultures.

My wife and I theorize that Paul mentioned the vision of four generations because after three generations is when the sins of the fathers are broken and reversed. When you have disciples multiplied beyond three generations you have a movement of God's Spirit and DNA that transforms cultures.

In the *Time* magazine article titled *Why Your DNA Isn't Your Destiny,* we read: "The new field of epigenetics is showing how your environment and your choices can influence your genetic code—and that of your kids."[iv]

The research in this article confirms that cultures can be changed by behavioral transformation. Getting back to the dinner table is about getting back to multiplying disciples with Christ-like modeling that will reach "all nations."

I love the scene in *The Lord of The Rings: The Fellowship of the Ring* where Boromir was admiring the Sword of Narsil (Aragorn's ancestor's sword).[v]

Aragorn appears and refers to it as "just a broken heirloom;" and while he puts it away it falls, and as he replaces it

Arwen appears and says to Aragorn: "Why do you fear the past? You are Isildur's heir...not Isildur himself...you are not bound to his fate."

Aragorn: "The same blood flows in my veins...the same weakness."

Arwen: "Your time will come....you will face the same evil and you will defeat it!" She then speaks in elvish tongue which translates to: "The shadow does not hold sway yet — not over you, not over me."

We can overcome the sins of our fathers and the pull of our culture by the power of God's Spirit if we will face our sin and poor choices, and do the right things for the right reasons, because *"Greater is He that is within us than he that is in the world"* (1 John 4:4)!

With the Greater One in us, we have the ability to reproduce His life to the fourth generation and beyond. Therefore, the sins of the fathers handed down to the third generation are broken by Jesus Christ. Jesus (The Tree of Life) will multiply His life in and through us, leaving a lasting legacy of multiplying disciples.

This is how ethnic groups or nations are transformed and curses are broken by the power of Jesus Christ. A lasting legacy is left from generation to generation as we multiply His life by making disciples, and connecting them with His family. It starts with you and me saying, "Here I am Lord, change me; send me; use me."

Reflection

Look at where we have come, or is it where we have gone? You may be old enough to reflect on the dinner table scenes around your favorite TV shows over the past four decades: *My Three Sons, Leave it to Beaver, the Waltons, Little House on the Prairie, Good Times, All in the Family*, then we shift to *NYPD Blue, Friends, Seinfeld, ER, Heroes, Lost* and then the reality shows that dominate TV today.

What has happened to the dinner table? I believe we can see the progressive loss of spiritual and relational vitality as time around the dinner table has diminished. At least on

Survivor you used to have to go through a food challenge to reconnect with your loved ones.

Though my wife would always tell me as we watched the food challenges on *Survivor*, "Sorry honey, if I had to eat gross stuff like that I would have to cry and wave goodbye to you." I find it interesting that she will eat all kinds of stuff with people of other cultures to keep from offending them and to share the love of our Creator; but she won't swallow a bug for me. Her priorities are totally messed up. LOL!

I certainly don't want to go back to some of those old TV shows, or to what some refer to as the "golden years." But I do want to connect with God and others, and I believe that this is sorely lacking in our culture, even among many who claim to be spiritual.

There is hope! Take a look at the perfect host and example at the dinner table…

Reflection

What did you like about this chapter?

What did you not understand?

What was challenging?

What does this chapter say about people in general?

What did you learn about God in this chapter?

What changes will you make because you read this chapter?

What do you want to share from this chapter?

Chapter 2
Jesus and the Divine Dinner

"The evening meal was being served, and the devil had already prompted Judas Iscariot, son of Simon, to betray Jesus. Jesus knew that the Father had put all things under his power, and that he had come from God and was returning to God; so he got up from the meal, took off his outer clothing, and wrapped a towel around his waist. After that, he poured water into a basin and began to wash his disciples' feet, drying them with the towel that was wrapped around him" (John 13:2-5, NIV).

Jesus was a model, or an exact representation of what it is to be the greatest in the Kingdom, *a servant*. In preparation for the Passover He modeled servant-hood for His disciples by washing their feet; and then shared with them a meal. At the dinner table He revealed to them a new covenant, we call the New Testament. In doing this, Jesus provided an example for how we are to do church as we are gathering and going.

His example to His disciples also showed them how to be family together—to actually be the church. He told them they were His family because they had committed to do the Father's will. When we arrive at John 13 in the upper room, He tells his followers that He is providing an example for them. He proceeds to serve them and wash their feet. This is an example of what it means to prophesy over others by washing their feet with the water of the word when we gather. (1 Corinthians 14; Ephesians 5)

As we go forth as God's sent ones, journeying in this world, our feet will get dirty. Remember we are in a battle, on a mission, and our feet must be fitted in the readiness of the Gospel of peace as we look for the person of peace. (Ephesians 6; Luke 10) So, when we gather, just like Christ's example in John 13, we need to share a covenant meal to remind us of who we are, and whose we are; and to wash one another's feet by speaking words that will strengthen, build up, and comfort each other. Christ provided a vision for change that would soon become a reality in the lives of his disciples.

Have you thought about how this was modeled by Jesus?

Are you following this model with other Christ-followers?

From my journal: Ethiopia, 2011

"One of the things that I've observed about this trip is how people are transformed around the dinner table or a coffee table. This observation further solidifies my views about God's kingdom and the need for his people to get back to the dinner table.

Part of the problems in the West is that we have lost our way to the dinner table (hospitality — Romans 12:13; 1 Peter 4:9). Even the Lord's Supper in most communities has become some religious snack instead of feasting on the remembrance of Christ's goodness as a full meal. It is symptomatic of us losing our way to God. Our all-consuming fast food culture is going to be the death of us, physically and spiritually."

A deeper look at the Lord's Supper: A Divine Dinner

For followers of Jesus Christ, one of the most important reproducible patterns for us to engage with other Christians in is the Lord's Supper, Communion, or the Eucharist. This ordinance is more than an institutional ceremony. It is an invitation to an intimate relationship and freedom.

When you read the Gospels' (Matthew, Mark, Luke and John) accounts of the Supper and understand the background story, you discover the sacred romance between a loving God and a rebellious people that He has relentlessly pursued and chosen as His beloved bride.

When Jesus was born, many had been waiting for years for a new manna (bread) from God that would change their hearts. Others had given up and begun to pursue religious laws created by man and political structures that they hoped would bring them power and security. In John 5:39 Jesus accuses some of these power brokers and religious leaders of worshipping the scriptures rather than the Author of them. Somehow, over time they had lost their way. They looked to their traditions and cultural customs to gain acceptance, security and significance.

Since the exodus in the Old Testament, the children of Israel had followed a Levitical system with a tabernacle (altar and tent). It eventually became a more permanent temple that was a pattern of an amazing reality that was to come. (Hebrews 10:1) Little did they know that over a divine dinner during the Passover celebration, the One who created the heart would reveal that the prophesied transformation of lives and hearts was at hand. Jesus prepared Himself and His followers for His sacrifice that would give us the right to be children of God by being born again.

As the One "who was, and is, and is to come," Jesus shared the new covenant that would remove sin and bring life to His disciples. Interestingly, the children of Israel were celebrating the Passover meal to commemorate their deliverance from slavery in Egypt. Jesus announced at this meal that the prophets' words of old have been realized and materialized before their very eyes. (Isaiah 53; Ezekiel 36; and Psalm 22) Hearts would be set free from slavery to sin through a relationship with Christ. It was now more than a mere shadow—it was a reality!

The tree of life, eternal life, is now possible through a relationship with Christ. He said the Kingdom of God is at hand and we are His servants. He is the King in His Kingdom. He uses an ordinary yet extraordinary meal to remind us of His rule in our hearts. He turns ordinary people into extraordinary servants in His Kingdom. However, too often the significance of this meal is reduced to a ritual that sustains life about as well as fast food sustains the body. Jesus Christ intended for His "last supper" to be the beginning of an intimate sharing of life together over a meal, and to serve as a reminder that the same life that sustains me, sustains you; and we must metabolize Christ together to really walk with God and advance His Kingdom.

This meal was a symbol of sustenance for now, as well as anticipation for the incredible life to come. It will be celebrated at the greatest banquet of all. Scripture calls it the "marriage supper of the Lamb". Many people view heaven as some static church service with angels on clouds playing boring music. It's no sterile place. Rather, it's a dynamic, *"new heaven and new earth."* (Matthew 26:28; Revelation 19:9)

I love what Frank Viola says about Christians' loss of the meaning of the Lord's Supper:

> "It's no longer the 'Lord's Supper.' Today's version would better be called the 'Savior's Sampler,' the 'Nazarene Niblet,' or the 'Lord's Appetizer.' Forgive the humor but can we really call a cracker crumb and a shot glass of grape juice a supper?"[vi]

The reason many of us (not everyone) in church don't experience being filled by God or satisfied in life is because we believe worship is something that we do in an hour, in a building on a Sunday. God's desire for us is so much more than that. He wants us to hunger and thirst for Him 24/7. The Father wants us to live a life of moment by moment worship. However, that is a lifestyle or a way of life, which must be maintained with good spiritual training, spiritual exercise and good nutrition.

It also means feasting on God's Word and fasting from the junk that makes us sick. There are no short cuts and there is no other way to know God. He is the Way and we are to be people of the Way. One of the simplest ways I know of doing this is to be involved with those who are living life within what Neil Cole calls a Life Transformation Group (or LTG group).[vii] LTG groups have three simple tasks of training:

1) Each member commits to read 30 chapters of Scripture a week in context.

2) Members confess sins and weaknesses.

3) LTG group members pray for others' lives to change as they are being changed.

LTG groups need not have a leader because members are committed learning how to love God, how to love people, and how to make "disciple-making disciples." Men meet with men; and women meet with women.

Another key to spiritual growth is for you to find a "spiritual parent," or mentor. This would be someone who is further along than you, who will agree to help you grow and mature in your relationship with God. Spiritual parenting is a core value in the Bible that was modeled by Jesus Himself. This is all done in the context of community or spiritual family.

If we had more organic communities as I'm proposing in this book this would happen automatically, and would not have to be programmed. Of course no one can change you; you must want to change in order to be changed. Spiritual growth (discipleship) is a holistic process that takes a village over time. Too many people view discipleship in a compartmentalized fashion, only as one on one, or only in a group of 12. I'm suggesting that it requires all the above, and more.

The more I read the Bible the more I am blown away at how we ignore the patterns and directions for our assemblies that Christ and His apostles laid out. These patterns were to be repeated as simple, reproducible reminders of Christ as the Head of His body and the Foundation of His dwelling place. The Lord's Supper for example:

> "Foreign though it may seem to the contemporary church, the first century church enjoyed the Lord's

Supper as a banquet that foreshadowed the Marriage Supper of the Lamb. It was not until after the close of the New Testament era that the Lord's Supper was altered from its pristine form. If that was indeed the practice of the early church, should we not follow their example?"[viii]

"From the beginning, the Last Supper was for Christians not an annual Christian Passover, but a regularly repeated meal in honor of the Lord."[ix]

"In the first century, the Lord's Supper included not only the bread and cup but an entire meal."[x]

In order for us to get back to the Lord's Table we will have to open our hearts and homes to the Lord.

The Story behind the meal:[xi]

When Jesus told his disciples to partake of the Lord's Supper "in remembrance of me," they were gathered at the Passover meal. This was a meal that the Jewish people had celebrated for centuries. The Passover celebration is the celebration of God's use of Moses and Aaron to deliver His people from the slavery and bondage of Egypt. The story is a foreshadowing of the reality to come that we would one day find our freedom from the slavery of sin through Jesus Christ, our Deliverer.

Moses in the Old Testament is a type of Christ, which means he gives us a glimpse of what Jesus Christ will look like as God in the flesh. Moses led the people from slavery in Egypt, through the baptism of the Red Sea, into a time of wandering in the wilderness and discovering the absolute need for trust and surrender that leads to the Promised Land that God had prepared for them.

Jesus Christ has made it possible for us to be delivered from our sin and when we are delivered from our sin we then must choose allegiance to him through baptism. It is also in the times of experiencing the wilderness and difficulty of life that we discover that this Christian life cannot be lived under our own strength. We need to absolutely trust and surrender to the power of God's Spirit within us, embrace our identity as children of God, in order for us to enter His rest (the Promised Land).

The Passover meal was a celebration of the deliverance from Egypt but also an anticipation of the One who was to come, the deliverer, and the perfect one. For seven days the Jews were instructed to eat only pure unleavened bread. During the Passover celebration preparation, the father would often send the children throughout the house trying to find any leaven inside. God is looking for a pure house to dwell. In the Bible, leaven or yeast symbolized sin and hypocrisy.

Unleavened bread eaten over a time of seven days symbolized a holy walk with the Lord. 1 Corinthians 5:7-8 says, "Get rid of the old yeast that you may be a new batch without yeast — as you really are. For Christ, our Passover lamb has been sacrificed. Therefore let us keep the Festival, not with the old yeast, the yeast of malice and wickedness, but with bread without yeast, the bread of sincerity and truth." The type of bread that was used during the Passover celebration meal is called matzah. When Jesus held up the matzah bread He said, "This is my body given for you, do this in remembrance of me." He was providing us an incredible picture of our Lord and Savior Jesus Christ's fulfillment of the foreshadowing of the reality to come.

The bread has visible stripes where it was cooked on a griddle. The prophet Isaiah said, *"By His stripes we are healed."* The bread also has holes in it and you can actually see through it. The Scripture says they shall look upon me who they have pierced. He was pierced for our transgressions. This bread was also pure because it was without yeast or without sin.

In addition, while celebrating the Passover meal, at the time that would be considered our dessert, it was tradition to hide three pieces of matzah under the table wrapped in white linen. The bread would have looked like a stack of three large crackers. At the same time, year after year, the father would pull the bread out from under the table (He is risen), grab the middle piece of the three wrapped in one (Father, Son and Holy Spirit), out from under the table and then he would begin to break off pieces and pass them around and say a blessing. The blessing was *"blessed are you, oh Lord, our God, King of the universe who brings forth bread from the earth."*

Jesus was telling His disciples that this bread is a symbol (a foreshadowing) of my sinless body that would be brought forth (resurrected) from the earth. He was communicating to His followers that He is a sinless sacrifice, and that we will be healed by His suffering because He will be pierced for our sins. He would be buried and resurrected; saying God will bring my body from the earth. He will fill a sinless dwelling place, a body (that the Father cleans up by the Son) where he is the cornerstone among livings stones as a foundation and He will function as the head. Remember, in John 12:24 Jesus said unless a kernel of wheat falls into the ground it will not reproduce life? (My paraphrase)

Think about these words from Jesus who describes himself as the *"bread of life."* He was born in Bethlehem which in Hebrews means the house of bread. The bread is an image of Jesus Christ. God fed the Israelites in the wilderness with manna from Heaven. Jesus Christ said that he is that manna from heaven that will feed and nourish us with His very life as we learn to metabolize Christ. Jesus revealed this to them, at this meal, after hundreds of years of men celebrating the Passover meal and telling the story. He was fulfilling all of the deepest longings that only a Savior and Lord can fill. He is the living Word from God that satisfies our deepest longings. He took the bread, raised it up, and said the "blessing," Jesus said, *"this is my body given to you, do this in remembrance of me."* After they partook of the bread at the Passover meal they would share a cup of wine.

In the Jewish culture wine was a symbol of covenant. It was used when the bridegroom was making a commitment or covenant with his bride. The bridegroom would approach his chosen bride with a contract, a covenant of marriage, which they both would sign. A price was paid called a dowry. After the covenant, or the agreement, was made the future bridegroom and the future bride would share a cup of wine that would seal the covenant.

Then the groom would then tell the bride, *"I am going to prepare a place for you"* and he would return to his father's house. Remember when Jesus said, *"I am going to prepare a place for you?"* The bridegroom's responsibility was to actually go and prepare a place where they would have their honeymoon. It would be a very special place for them to live. A place that was set apart, bought with a price. The place the bridegroom prepared was the place where the marriage would be consummated and celebrated. Another fascinating note is the fact that only the bridegroom's father could give the final call as to when the marriage house was complete, and prepared for the consummation and celebration of the marriage.

While the Bridegroom was making all of these preparations; the future bride was waiting in anticipation. Eager to be married, and waiting for her bridegroom's return, she would keep herself pure. She would keep an oil lamp lit with plenty of oil standing by; for her groom could return at any time. As a matter of fact, part of the tradition was for the bridegroom to return in the middle of the night as a surprise. When the father gave his approval upon completion of their home; the bridegroom and his groomsman would sneak over to the bride's home to steal her away.

The bridegroom could not just come in and grab up his bride without a warning, there had to be a shout! Someone in the bridegroom's party would shout out, "behold the bridegroom comes!" Then the bride and the bride's party would quickly trim their lamps and return with the bridegroom.

Meanwhile, back at the place that had been prepared for them by the bridegroom under the supervision of his father, there would be the *"cloud of many witnesses,"* the father and the wedding party. They would be gathered and assembled waiting for the marriage celebration, which would not begin until there was consummation of the marriage.

The bridegroom would take his beautiful bride into his marriage chambers and consummate the marriage. He would pour his life into her and she would welcome and receive the life he was giving. The bridegroom's best friend would stand by the door and listen for the groom's voice, telling him that the marriage was consummated and official. Then the crowd would enjoy the festivities of a seven-day celebration. The celebration was concluded with a feast—"The marriage supper of The Lamb."

Our Lord's Supper today is to be a celebration of the incredible good news, the Gospel. It is the story of God's sacred Romance, His pursuit of a bride, His desire to dwell and live among us in a covenant relationship. Jesus is our bridegroom and we are His bride. He has approached us with a new contract, a new covenant. He stated, *"this is the blood of the new covenant shed for many for the forgiveness of sins."* He paid a dowry price that was so high, He even said, *"Father, remove this cup from me but not my will but your will."* He paid the price for His bride upon the cross when He died for our sins. Jesus told His bride, the Church, *"I go and prepare a place for you."*

Only the father knows when the bridegroom will come for us but we are to wait in purity, set apart, prepared for His return. When He returns there will be a shout and a trumpet blast. There will be an incredible consummation and celebration as we participate in the marriage supper of The Lamb.

The Lord's Supper is intended to be a celebration of the anticipated great day of consummation; as well as a commemoration *("do this in remembrance of me")* of what Christ has done for us so we can be, and do, what He has called us to. We are a new race, a family that has been given a mission. We are to express His spiritual DNA (His life) in our everyday lives together. This is why the Lord's Supper was most frequently observed in homes, in the New Testament. This is also why we need to get back to hospitality if we are going to get back to the dinner table where Christ transforms lives.

Reflection

"Then he took the cup, gave thanks and offered it to them, saying, 'Drink from it, all of you. This is my blood of the covenant, which is poured out for many for the forgiveness of sins. I tell you, I will not drink of this fruit of the vine from now on until that day when I drink it anew with you in my Father's kingdom.' When they had sung a hymn, they went out to the Mount of Olives.

He gave thanks: 'Blessed are you, O Lord our God, King of the universe, Creator of the fruit of the vine.' He took the cup and lifted it up and said this blessing, 'This is his blood of the covenant, which is poured out for many for the forgiveness of sins.'"
(Matthew 26:27-29, NKJV)

Throughout the Old Testament we see stories and images of the pursuit of a bride. This serves as incredible foreshadowing of the sacred romance. The Gospel is the greatest love story of all time. It's a Bridegroom and His pursuit of a bride, ending with an incredible celebration supper—the party of the ages, mentioned in Revelation 19:9 as *"the marriage supper of the Lamb!"*

Reflection

What did you like about the chapter?

What did you not understand?

What was challenged you most?

What does this chapter say about people in general?

What did you learn about God in this chapter?

What changes will you make because you read this chapter?

What do you want to share from this chapter?

Chapter 3
Hospitality By Guy and Kelli Caskey

Do you find yourself saying, "Let's *go to* church?" Most of us agree that the church is not a building. It is a gathering of believers. Have we forgotten who we are? Have we forgotten the way to *be the church* (His bride or body). It appears to me that we have, and for one important reason. We have lost our spirit of hospitality? Why would the Lord command us in His Word to be hospitable if it were optional?

A pastor once told me that he did not open his home to others because hospitality was not his gift. What part of 1 Peter 4:9, which says *"be hospitable to one another,"* does one not understand? Where is it referred to as "a gift?" The incredible movement of Christianity recorded in the book of Acts, which changed countless lives and turned the world upside down, was often called "The Way." Christ was another type of King. Christ the Way had come to establish a new people, and a new movement. It spread from house to house, city to city, and nation to nation through the hospitality of His people.

The foundation of Christ's movement didn't remain in the temple. It was laid in homes, with pockets of people who committed their allegiance to Him. It appears that they gave not only their lives, but their homes to be used for gatherings to support the movement; to disciple new believers; and to lovingly host journeying strangers. *"For I was hungry and you gave me something to eat, I was thirsty and you gave me something to drink, I was a stranger and you invited me in, I needed clothes* and you clothed me, I was sick and you looked after me..." (Matthew 25:35-36, NIV).

What about these verses?

> "Now the overseer must be above reproach, the husband of but one wife, temperate, self-controlled, respectable, hospitable, able to teach" (1 Timothy 3:2, NIV).
>
> "Rather he must be hospitable, one who loves what is good, who is self-controlled, upright, holy and disciplined" (Titus 1:8, NIV).
>
> "Share with God's people who are in need. Practice hospitality." (Rom 12:13, NIV).
>
> "Offer hospitality to one another without grumbling" (1 Peter 4:9, NIV).

There is a strong connection between the loss of our vision and mission, and the loss of hospitality. One of my favorite quotes supports this:

> "If every Christian family in the world simply offered good conversation around a table once a week to neighbors, *we would eat our way into the kingdom of God.*"[xii] (Emphasis mine)

I was reared in a culture often praised for its "southern hospitality." But sometimes, unfortunately, what is known as *southern hospitality* is sometimes little more than an external front that covers up underlying criticism, arrogance and fear. *Southern hospitality* sometimes appears as the stereotyped big haired lady with the broad smile who calls you, "honey." One might not know if they aren't from around here, that what she really wants is for you to eat and leave so she can continue gossiping with her friends. If you read the book, or saw the movie, *"The Help,"* then you understand that stereotype and its inauthentic hospitality.[xiii]

True hospitality emanates from the heart. It serves as a place of healing. The word "hospital" is a word within the word **hospital***ity*. However, some hospitals, which are supposed to be places of care and healing, have instead become institutions focused on profit, not people. God's design is for our homes to be Christ-centered havens of healing.

If our homes are not places of healing, is Christ (the Healer and Great Physician) really at the center of our lives? One does not have to be perfect to be Christ-centered. We simply need to be committed to the process of growing in Christ-likeness. True hospitality is seen in one whose heart is open to God, and others. Loving God, and loving people is at the core of Kingdom DNA, and hospitality is evidence of it.

Consider These Practical Ways to Practice Hospitality

1. Open your home for someone to live with you.

For 20 of our 23 years of marriage, Kelli and I have had someone living with us. I could not begin to count the number of Christ-centered gatherings and meals we've enjoyed in our home. It has truly been a place of blessing for many. Please understand, this has not been easy. We have learned many valuable lessons on this journey of practicing hospitality. Our friend Greg Carlet shares:

> Hospitality, practically shown to me, is how I experienced God's love and acceptance of me.
>
> A few years ago, due to some unfortunate circumstances, I found myself at the lowest point of my life. My world had been turned upside down, and I was devastated. I believed in God, but I definitely did not understand why He was allowing certain things to happen. Sometimes I was angry. Sometimes I was sad. And sometimes I was both at the same time. It was during this time that God chose to show His love to me in a unique and tangible way.
>
> One day, seemingly out of nowhere, I received an invitation that I was not expecting. This invitation would end up becoming a two-year, life-changing experience. I was invited to move in with the Caskey family and, in a very real sense, to become a part of their family. But this was not just about having a roof over my head, although I was definitely grateful for that. This was an invitation to join them around the table for meals, to spend holidays with them, to have many deep and meaningful conversations with them, and to have them speak into my life and into the lives of my children.
>
> Over the course of the next two years, I went from feeling alone and rejected, wondering what in the world just happened, to feeling loved and accepted. Their home was truly a place of care and healing. It was like an emotional and spiritual hospital and rehabilitation center all rolled into one.

Not only was I constantly pointed to God and to seek Him first, but I was challenged to grow and change and not just stay stuck in the same place I had been in previous years.

I am grateful to be one of the many people to whom Guy and Kelli have opened their home and lives.

One thing we have learned about having people live with us is the need for clearly defined expectations and boundaries. We have also learned the importance of spending time in prayer, and considering the details around who we will invite to live with us.

Who will live with us? Nothing is more important than that. We have three children, and because of that, there are many details for us to consider. When our two daughters were middle to high school aged, we were obviously not going to invite a teenage boy to live with us. We most often chose young men in their mid to late 20's. These were young men who had demonstrated a desire to grow in their relationship with Christ, and who wanted to be discipled and mentored by us. I'll address this commitment in our contract which we will discuss next. When selecting our extended house-guests, we considered their age, gender, maturity, and their desire to grow.

Our Contract

We have used and recommend a contract be written and signed when opening your home to an extended house-guest. A contract establishes and helps everyone involved know the expectations and responsibilities of each party. Our shift to the use of a contract came from having made a lot of mistakes in the early days by failing to consider important details. We were young, naïve, and inexperienced. We thought all of the details of our hosting arrangement could be considered and communicated along the way.

However, it's quite different. You see, each party will have their own filters and views of what the relationship should be. A contract serves as a constant, or a compass to check when we lose our way. In addition to that, there are also practical things like how to handle food, when to do the laundry, etc. Below is a sample contract that we used in our home. Some of the details will change from person to person but overall, this is a good example of what we've used:

Contract for Living with the Caskey's
___/___/___

I understand that I am entering into a relationship with the Caskeys that involves me becoming part of their family. I am responsible to make my own decisions. However, while I am living in their home, I give the Caskeys permission be involved in my life by pointing out what the Bible says about the situations and decisions I will be making.

Financial responsibilities:
1. I agree to pay the Caskeys $_____ per month for rent, utilities and groceries. This payment will be made in either two (2) equal parts on the 1st and 15th of each month; or one (1) payment of $_____ at the beginning of each month. **The first payment is due: ___/___/___.**

2. I will pay for my own toiletry items such as shampoo, deodorant, medication, and etc.

3. I will purchase any special food or drink on my own.

4. This contract is good for one year ending __/__/___.

Other:

1. I agree to pick up after myself in all common areas especially my bathroom. I will also act as part of the family by helping to set the table and clean up the kitchen after dinner when I eat dinner here.

2. I will fully clean the bathroom, including the shower/tub area once a month.

3. If I won't be home for dinner I will communicate with the Caskeys as far in advance as possible.

4. If I plan to stay away from home over night I will communicate that with the Caskeys. If it is a last minute decision I will text one of the Caskeys cell phones so they will not be worried in the morning.

5. I agree to communicate openly if I have been hurt, and to sincerely apologize if I have hurt

someone. I agree to maintain open communication through difficulties and not shut down.

6. I understand that Sunday will be my day to do laundry. If I need to use the washer or dryer at other times I will ask Kelli for permission.

7. I will not adjust the central air or heat without talking to Guy.

8. When Kelli returns home after grocery shopping, I will help her unload her car and put them away. I will also occasionally run to the store to help out the family.

Print Your
Name_____
Date __/__/____.

_____ Signed

_____ Signed
Guy Caskey   Date __/__/____.

_____ Signed
Kelli Caskey   Date __/__/____.

2. **Host a biblical community**

In Biblical *ekklesia* hospitality is an essential factor in building Community. God will use someone who is hospitable to reach

Commented [CL11]: Should you make a note or brie this word for your audience?

their friends and neighbors; to help disciple, train, and equip other Christ-followers; and to host Christ centered gatherings (church). The host homes provide an environment for people to experience a healing community. If we want to effectively use our homes the first thing we need to do is give them to God. They are His homes and we are to be good stewards of them for His sake.

In addition, we need to be open and receptive to being used by God. At the time of the meeting, greet people at the door with a warm, welcoming smile. This communicates a lot about your heart for hospitality. Strangely, some of us struggle with this because it feels fake to us. It's important to remember, it is not fake to be who God wants you to be no matter how you feel. God has given you joy, and a challenge to be hospitable. So, for you to be who God desires you to be is not fake. In God's eyes you are in Christ and the more you see yourself that way the more you will become like Him.

On the other hand, sadly, some claim to be Christ-followers and then treat people poorly by displaying bad body language, being distant and aloof when people are in their homes. Being an introvert or shy is fine. However, it is no excuse for this kind of behavior. Whether we are introverts or extroverts, we each need to stretch and grow to be like Christ. That's what it means for us to be transformed by the renewing of our minds as Paul instructs is in Romans 12:1-3. For us to be transformed we will need to open our lives to God and others.

Hospitality is a demonstration of Christ's love to others. Our homes need not be perfect. However, there are certainly some practical things we can do to make them warm and inviting. The main thing is that we welcome people with

Christ's love, rather than worry about the place where we are meeting.

Because of its importance, we thought it would be good to describe a hospitable host home like those we have used in the past for a Body of Christ Gathering.

The host home should have drinking glasses and plates available when people start to arrive. We ask each host to provide beverages and the Lord's Supper supplies for the group/church each week. This need not be anything expensive. Iced tea, water or lemonade, or coffee is great. (Provide whatever fits your budget.) Refreshments/meals are symbols of sharing life together. Important encouraging and crucial conversations take place during the sharing of a meal.

It is best if the host welcomes guests at the door and directs them to where to put their belongings; where the restrooms are; where the refreshments are being served; and to communicate any house rules, etc. It is very important that the host be warm and friendly to each guest. It can be the one thing that makes someone want to come back. Please consider these things before you commit to be a host home. The commitment to be a host home is a serious consideration.

Practical suggestions for hosting a group/church

Check the thermostat. Some say that 67 degrees Fahrenheit is the ideal temperature for groups. Remember, the addition of a few people along with the use of the stove or oven, in a home, will increase the ambient temperature. We set the temperature at our house at 70 during the summer and 65-67 during the winter. Of course, you may be gathering in a place where there is no air conditioning and that is just fine. Some of my greatest gathering experiences were in Ethiopia where life is simple and there is no air conditioning. However, in August in Houston, Texas where we live, A/C is much appreciated! (Smile)

Sniff around. We sometimes become accustomed to, and overlook the odors in our homes, but visitors will sense them immediately. Pets, things children spill in odd places, heavy perfumes, the evening dinner, even room deodorizers can irritate noses. Consider lighting a few scented candles, or simmering some potpourri on the stove. Research shows, for instance, that the fragrance of peppermint helps keep people alert.

Let your light shine, but not too brightly. Low lamplights are better than bright florescent or overhead lighting. The room should be bright enough for everyone to read, yet low enough to feel cozy.

Guard against distractions. Encourage everyone to turn off their cell phones. Put pets in another room or outside. Turn off TV sets, radios and computers during the meeting. Sometimes, it's best to keep certain dogs with the group, if they are more distracting when put outside or kenneled. Animals can be challenging. Remember, not everyone is comfortable with animals. Some are allergic to them. Very few of my Ethiopian friends in Africa allow dogs inside their houses. So they are shaking their heads at this time.

We do not expect perfection from our host homes. We only ask that each of us commit to continually grow and learn new ways we can serve others with our homes. God wants to use our homes as places others can come and grow in their relationship with Christ, or possibly meet Christ for the first time.

Have the home where everyone wants to be

It may sound like a crazy statement but it is true. You know the house where all the teenagers like to hang out? I remember that house when I was growing up. Of course that can be true for good reasons, and sometimes, not so good reasons. However, when our kids were still young, we decided that we wanted to know their friends. So as they grew, we would do things in such a way that their friends would want to be at our house. Below is a list of things we have done in our 23 years of marriage to make our home inviting to others. These are only examples. Each person, family and home is unique so you will need to find what makes sense for your family, home, and budget.

1. From renting our first apartment through buying each house, we have considered the location and set up of the living rooms, and parking. We always asked the question, "Could we host a group here?" This has been a deciding factor for all of our homes. In addition, if you plan to have someone live with you, you will want to take this a step further. The home we currently own allows us to have men use one separate bathroom and shower; and the girls have their own. I realize this is not possible for everyone; however, these are the type of details to think about when you are making these decisions.

2. As you are financially able, invest in games, ping pong table, etc. We have had as many as 50 youth, consisting of five small groups and a large gathering time, meeting in our home each week. We bought a basketball goal and a trampoline. Both were a hit and many good times and conversations were had. This also attracted our children's

friends to our house. When we were less financially able, we made sure to have simple things like cards, table games, or Dominoes to play.

3. We suggest that you invest in a set of coffee cups and a coffee pot. One thing I have learned in Texas and Ethiopia is that almost everyone loves a good cup of coffee. Some of my best conversations have been over cups of coffee. Invite a neighbor, or maybe a stay-at-home mom who is struggling to your home. Invite a young couple over who needs someone to talk to about their marriage. Having coffee is a less expensive way to extend hospitality than is providing a meal. So if you are on a tight budget, this is a great way to entertain people. Of course coffee isn't the only beverage to use. You know your audience, so do what works for your relationships.

Warnings

The perfect home, the perfect circumstances

Forget the need to have the perfect home, or a certain amount of money to be hospitable. This is a lie. I (Kelli) was deeply convicted of this falsehood when I was at a training one year. The speaker told a story of a woman who had a group of people over to her very small home for dinner. She had everything prepared nicely, and after much fun and lively conversations, some of her guests offered to help clean up. She resisted and they relented. Later the speaker found out that the reason she would not allow them help her clean house was because she had no running water. She was embarrassed that she had to take the dishes outside to the clean them. The point of the story was, she used what little she had to bless others and didn't let things get in the way of being obedient and serving others.

This convicted me. When we were newly married we lived in a very small apartment-like home. Our furniture was hand-me-downs that really didn't match; and we barely had enough money to provide food for ourselves. I learned that night at the training that I was worried about the wrong things. There are always ways for us to be hospitable with the resources we have.

It reminds me of the three people who brought their offering. Two gave out of their excess, but the old woman gave one coin, which was all she had. God said she was the one who was blessed because she gave all she had, though it didn't seem like much. She gave it *all*.

Décor versus relationship

One additional thing that I (Kelli) spent years concerned about with was the idea that things had to be perfect when people came over. This does not matter. I would spend hours cleaning and making sure everything was just so. The napkins had to match the paper plates, etc. This was an exhausting waste of energy. Once I finally realized this, the experience was more fun and much less stressful.

There were times when I had no energy left to entertain my guests by the time they arrived because I had spent it all on the décor. What a waste. I asked myself, "Do you look at people's floors when you go to their house? Do you notice small things being out on the counter? Was the conversation better or was it more fun because the napkins matched the plates?" "No," was the answer to those questions. As a matter of fact, other than sweeping/vacuuming up dog hair, I *never* clean the floor now before people come over. Forget mopping.

I realized that mopping is for *after* the gathering when it's a mess.

A House is a home, not a museum.

This is another excellent lesson I (Kelli) have learned through the years. Have you ever been to someone's home where you felt like you shouldn't sit on the couch, or touch anything? You know, one of those homes where you put your children on leashes (not literally) because if they moved they may break something? This is not the kind of home you want or need in order to be hospitable. Please hear me. There is nothing wrong with nice things, but consider these things when you decorate your home if you plan to be a host. On the other hand, you don't want your home to be so un-kempt that people are afraid to sit down, or touch anything because they may get dirty.

Someone paid me the greatest compliment once, when they said, "Kelli, your home is comfortable." I've always wanted a home that was inviting and cozy. It made my day to hear that we had achieved such an atmosphere. Homes that have this kind of atmosphere can lead to life-changing connections that lead to transformation as we point people to Christ together in community. This transformation occurs when we learn to put Christ at the center of everything we do as "the Vine" and metabolize His life.

Reflection

What did you like about the chapter?

What did you not understand?

What was challenging?

What does this chapter say about people in general?

What did you learn about God in this chapter?

What changes will you make because you read this chapter?

What do you want to share from this chapter?

Chapter 4
Metabolize

"I am the bread of life. Your forefathers ate the manna in the desert, yet they died. But here is the bread that comes down from heaven, which a man may eat and not die. I am the living bread that came down from heaven. If anyone eats of this bread, he will live forever. This bread is my flesh, which I will give for the life of the world" (John 6:48-51, NIV).

Becoming like Christ:

Conversion is more than a change of direction. It's a change in connection that leads to the transformation of life.

The term *metabolism*, derived from the Greek language, means "change" or "transformation". It relates to various processes within the body that convert food and other substances to energy and other metabolic byproducts the body uses. Metabolism is the building block for every cell in our bodies. It is a necessary function that allows our bodies to use food and other resources to maintain their working parts; to repair damage; to heal injuries; and to rid the body of toxins. In other words, metabolism is a necessary process, without which living organisms will die.

> **Commented [CL13]:** Perhaps this should be cited?

When we come to Christ for salvation, we change our allegiance and our connection. As part of the world system, our connection was with Adam. We were dead in our sins. We displayed (or expressed) the values of division and separation. Our loyalties were to race, gender, geo-political affiliation, or patriotism. However, once we are in Christ as new creations, we are members of a new race, where there is no longer gentile or Jew, male or female, American or Russian, etc. We become citizens of heaven--a new race!

For us to live and function properly, as new creations in Christ, we must learn to metabolize Christ. We must allow Him to be both the source and the nourishment of our lives. He alone can provide the spiritual energy we require to live the lives we are designed to live as *"new creations."*

Metabolizing the life of Christ starts with the realization that Jesus is the *Tree of Life*. He said, *"I am the vine you are the branches apart from me you can do nothing."* God's great desire is to see us come together around Christ, and allow His life to flow in and through us. He wants each of us to express the life of Christ to the world. This is important at the individual, and at the community level. So what does that mean for us?

For one thing, we need biblical *shepherds* who will lead sheep (i.e. people) to green pastures so they can feed and care for themselves rather than spoon- or bottle-feed them with milk. These leaders will teach them to feed themselves.

We need *evangelists* who will model for us what it means to go into the fields and reach the unreached, who will become our future leaders.

We need *teachers* who will teach people, to teach others how to spiritually feed themselves. God wants new believers (spiritual babes in Christ) to be strengthened so they can grow to maturity and strengthen others. This is God's design. Each of us in the kingdom of God is responsible to teach others. As individuals are strengthened, the body of Christ is strengthened as well. Each believer is to feed on the *"Tree of Life"* (Christ).

When we as individuals metabolize Christ's life something beautiful and transformational happens. Christ is revealed and expressed more fully when we gather. There are three places in Scripture that affirm this truth of our metabolizing Christ. They are John chapter six, chapter 15; and Hebrews chapter five. Let's look at them briefly.

> **Commented [CL15]:** spelling numbers or using numerals should be consistent here and throughout; perhaps your using the less than 10, more than 10 rule?

In the sixth chapter of John, after Jesus feeds the 5,000 and walks on water, He seeks a place of solitude. However, He has difficulty getting away because of the masses. Throngs of people are chasing him like today's paparazzi's, and celebrity autograph-chasers. He explains to them that He is the bread of life, the manna from Heaven bringing life.

Then he declares something quite strange. He says, *"But anyone who eats my flesh and drinks my blood has eternal life, and I will raise that person at the last day."* Some have erroneously interpreted this to mean that Jesus was encouraging cannibalism. He was saying that we need to metabolize Him (symbolically) as the tree of life and the bread of life who sustains our lives and energizes our spirits.

> **Commented [CL16]:** Scripture reference?

> *"As the living father sent me and I live because of the father, so whoever feeds on me, he also will live because of me. This is the bread that came down from heaven not like the bread that the fathers ate and died. Whoever feeds on this bread will live forever."*

> **Commented [CL17]:** Scripture reference?

This was not a reference to physical cannibalism at all. It was about a spiritual connection to our Creator, who designed each of us with a God-shaped gap (an energy void) within our lives that must be filled. By dying on the cross for our sins, Jesus made it possible for us to be cleansed of our sins, and filled with His Holy Spirit thus fulfilling our eternal destiny as the dwelling place of God.

God's temple isn't a building made with hands. We are God's temple, His church, the *ekklesia* of God; people in whom His very life resides and is manifested. It starts with our saying, "God help me, fill me, change me, and make me the man or woman you have designed me to be. I need you more than life, more than bread or water. You, more than anything or anyone in this world, can meet my deepest need."

In John chapter 15, Jesus and His followers had been modeling church together for almost three years. I have provided for you an example that must be reproduced. Think about this:

- What did this look like?
- What did it feel like to be a part of this body life?
- How did it function?
- How can we keep Him at the center?
- Why are we not following Jesus' modeling of church life?
- Why does Jesus say they would be even more effective when He went away?

Jesus said that He is the Vine (The Tree of Life) and we are the branches. He tells us that apart from Him we can do nothing of spiritual and eternal value. He described a process of growth that takes us from no fruit, to fruit, to more fruit, to much fruit-- *abundant fruit!* When a mature community of

Christ-followers trusts the Holy Spirit by looking to Christ (the Tree of Life), a connection will be made with the Divine that will produce abundant lasting fruit! They will experience unconditional love for one another that is only produced by Christ himself. Mature spiritual mothers and fathers will arise who have learned to metabolize Christ's life by learning and applying His Word through life's challenges; by practicing spiritual disciplines; and by remaining connected no matter the circumstances. They will have become contagious models of Christ likeness who will help the body grow to maturity.

There will be reproduction and the expression of Christ's life demonstrated through this community. Jesus was telling his first organic church (His disciples) that He was taking them to the garden again where they would be restored and nourished by Him, the "Tree of Life." They would be no longer cut off but connected to His nourishing life. (Genesis 2-3)

When we believe in our hearts and confess with our mouth's we become new creations who are spiritual babes. God's desire is for us then to grow to maturity into strong Christ-followers.

Those who buy into the lie that it is someone else's job to feed us on this journey become trapped in a state of continual infancy. Hebrew 5:11-14, NIV says it like this:

> *"We have much to say about this, but it is hard to explain because you are slow to learn. In fact, though by this time you ought to be teachers, you need someone to teach you the elementary truths of God's word all over again. You need milk, not solid food! Anyone who lives on milk, being still an infant, is not acquainted with the teaching about*

> *righteousness. But solid food is for the mature, who by constant use have trained themselves to distinguish good from evil."*

This reminds of the disturbing image of the four- or five-year-old boy in the movie, *Grown-Ups*, starring Adam Sandler who was still breast feeding![xiv] One reason we have so many people in the body of Christ who have character issues is because so few can feed themselves. They've not learned to, "train or discipline themselves." They do not know the difference between good and evil, which is a character flaw. Without metabolizing and applying biblical information there can be no transformation.

As Romans 12 says, every Christ-follower should be transformed by the renewing of his or her mind, and by total surrender to the Lordship of Christ. We will experience our perfect spiritual act of worship as we yield to God's direction. Unfortunately, for various reasons, this is the place, like in John chapter six, when many disciples choose to no longer follow and turn back. There is a clear difference between a fan and a follower. Once again, most of us would rather be fans of Jesus than truly pay the price to follow Him. In order to follow Christ we must metabolize Him!

A disciple of Christ is one who truly metabolizes Him. God said that we cannot be Christ's disciples unless we:

- Abide in Christ, are obedient, bearing fruit, glorifying God, have joy and love community - God's family. (John 15:7-17)
- Love others as Christ loves. (John 13:34-35)
- Are committed to praying, going/sending as disciples into unreached fields or pockets of people where there

are lost sheep and wolves. (Matthew 9:36-38; Luke 10:2)
- Are committed to Christ's teachings and His freedom. (John 8:31)
- Put Christ before self, family, and possessions. (Luke 14:25-35)
- Are willing to deny self, take up a cross daily, and follow Him. (Luke 9:23-25)
- Develop Christ like humility. (Philippians 2)
- Become a mature servant who is a gift to the body and equips it to serve. (Ephesians 4:11-16)

It's rare to find this level of disciple, one who has truly developed into *"the greatest in the Kingdom,"* who has a big enough vision to think small. As Francis Chan stated in a personal interview,

> *"I could fill my whole time doing interviews, speaking to crowds, and there's this natural human tendency because of our culture to think that the more people I talk to, the bigger the impact I'll have, and yet Jesus didn't spend His time just speaking to the masses. He spent the bulk of his time with a small group of people."*[xv]

Jesus said that the greatest in His Kingdom would be known as a servant (a disciple is a servant). In John chapter 13 Jesus provided an example of servanthood, then told His disciples to wait for the power that will come from Him to make it possible for them to do what He had done and even greater things than He had done.

Mature servants in the body will help others metabolize Christ and grow into mature servants. They will strengthen others through vision casting, by being an example, and by speaking words of encouragement and comfort.

I agree with Neil Cole's view on the biblical roles of elders and deacons, as described in 1 Timothy chapter 3; these are roles or functions that all Christ-followers should desire to develop. This describes a level of character and maturity for us all. It is a description of what it looks like to be a mature servant or *"the greatest in the Kingdom."*

> **Commented [CL18]:** I looked for an article or something on cmaresources.org but couldn't find anything specific; I think should note something simple like, for more on Neil Cole's view the biblical roles of elders and deacons, see X (please suggest blog, essay/article, etc.)

I see this letter from the Apostle Paul to his spiritual son Timothy, also an apostle, to remind him of how the family or "household of God" should function as a body or dwelling place. As I've said, for this to happen there must be mature spiritual mothers and fathers (elders) in the local context; and proven servants/equippers (deacons) who are the greatest in the Kingdom who serve multiple bodies of Christ in various locations, a trans-local context (five-fold ministers). These mature Christ-followers who effectively metabolize Christ's life will help others (the body) grow and mature. If we will stop looking at these roles as job descriptions, and see them as character descriptions for us all, we will see a more mature body develop.

> *"The same goes for those who want to be servants in the church: serious, not deceitful, not too free with the bottle, not in it for what they can get out of it. They must be reverent before the mystery of the faith, not using their position to try to run things. Let them prove themselves first. If they show they can do it, take them on. No exceptions are to be made for women — same qualifications: serious, dependable,*

not sharp-tongued, not overfond of wine. Servants in the church are to be committed to their spouses, attentive to their own children, and diligent in looking after their own affairs. Those who do this servant work will come to be highly respected, a real credit to this Jesus-faith.

I hope to visit you soon, but just in case I'm delayed, I'm writing this letter so you'll know how things ought to go in God's household, this God-alive church, bastion of truth. This Christian life is a great mystery, far exceeding our understanding, but some things are clear enough:

He appeared in a human body, was proved right by the invisible Spirit, was seen by angels. He was proclaimed among all kinds of peoples, believed in all over the world, taken up into heavenly glory" (1 Timothy 3:8-16, MSG).

These mature servants will help others on the journey identify proper seasons (like fasting, sending, etc.) in the development of the individual and the community (body).

Reflection

What did you like about the chapter?

What did you not understand?

What was challenging?

What does this chapter say about people in general?

What did you learn about God in this chapter?

What changes will you make because you read this chapter?

What do you want to share from this chapter?

Chapter 5
Fasting and Feasting

In the biblical narrative, the story of God's love, we find His people both fasting and feasting. One is in times of celebration, and the other is in times of anticipation. There were times for breaking bread (feasting); and there were times for breaking chains (fasting). Wise mature servants understand the times, the rhythms, and the seasons of life. Discerning the seasons is like knowing when to dance, and when to plant. An experienced mature farmer will be able to tell the difference.

Jesus did not say, "If *you fast....*" when He gave His disciples instruction for appropriate fasting. He said, "When *you fast...*", using the illustration of a bridegroom and bride in Hebrew culture. The bridegroom would feast with the bride before he left to prepare a place for her. While he was away, in a season of preparation, there was fasting and anticipation. When He returned there would be an incredible feast called "the marriage supper."

Seasons in our lives will come and go, ebb and flow. We as God's people should learn to discern them as His Spirit leads.

"Then John's disciples came and asked him, "How is it that we and the Pharisees fast, but your disciples

do not fast?" Jesus answered, "How can the guests of the bridegroom mourn while he is with them? The time will come when the bridegroom will be taken from them; then they will fast" (Matthew 9:14-15, NIV).

Fasting is for both the individual and the community. It is up to both to discern when the time for fasting should come and go. This is why discipleship and Christ-like maturity are so important. Wise decisions that determine one's destiny are motivated by a surrendered heart. In our network of churches and nonprofits we usually observe two 30 day fasts each year to pray over the entire network.

There are also seasons where each of the churches and non-profit ministries fast separately, when they feel the Lord is asking them to. We encourage individuals to fast for breakthroughs as the Spirit leads them. Whether it is fasting for a breakthrough for a family member or a friend who is far from God; or fasting for a personal breakthrough related to an issue of one's character, service or a difficulty he or she is facing; there will be times where each of us will need to see God come through in an area of our lives. In Scripture, we see those who fasted in the Old Testament, like Moses, Daniel and others. New Testament people who were known to fast include Jesus, Paul, Barnabas, the church in Antioch, and others. Fasting, which helps us grow in intimacy with God, should be a time when we focus on Him. The idea is to do without something (fast) that usually requires our attention, and focus instead on God.

During biblical times, preparing food and drink took a great deal of time. Therefore, to fast or go without food and drink, meant that the preparation time could be spent focusing on God. When hunger and thirst rise up they are reminders of our need to hunger and thirst for Him.

I often encourage people to take technology fasts by going without screens, TV, PC, Apple products, Facebook, Instagram, Pinterest, Twitter, etc. Fasting from food is still a great option, but there may be more time wasted on technology. Fasting can be an incredible time of transformation for us if we respond in humility with brokenness and true repentance. It can deepen our prayer life and bring about personal and corporate renewal.

Feasting on the other hand, for we Americans, is exemplified by our national Thanksgiving holiday. Thanksgiving is a time of faith, family, and great food. Thanksgiving, for God's people, should be a celebration of God's abundant provision and a reminder that we must trust Christ when there is abundance, and trust Him when our cupboards are bare.

One of the most quoted passages of Scripture is Philippians 4:13 which says: *"I can do all things through Christ..."* The context of this verse is actually about learning to trust God's power whether we have little or plenty. It's about being content. So whether we are feasting or fasting we can trust Christ and be content. *"Godliness with contentment is great gain"* (1 Timothy 6:6).

The great thing about feasting is that everyone can contribute to the shared meals where we celebrate our life together. Feasting is a reminder that we can do more together than we can do alone. I love the African proverb that says, "If you want to go fast, go alone; if you want to go far, go together."

In feasting we celebrate our journey together as God's people, moving forward, trusting Him to do all things, in and through us. A local gathering of the body of Christ should exemplify what it means to feast, often as it shares in the Lord's Supper.

Reflection

"When you fast, do not look somber as the hypocrites do, for they disfigure their faces to show men they are fasting. I tell you the truth, they have received their reward in full. But when you fast, put oil on your head and wash your face, so that it will not be obvious to men that you are fasting, but only to your Father, who is unseen; and your Father, who sees what is done in secret, will reward you" (Matthew 6:16-18, NIV).

"Then John's disciples came and asked him, "How is it that we and the Pharisees fast, but your disciples do not fast?" Jesus answered, "How can the guests of the bridegroom mourn while he is with them? The time will come when the bridegroom will be taken from them; then they will fast" (Matthew 9:14-15, NIV).

"Shout it aloud, do not hold back. Raise your voice like a trumpet. Declare to my people their rebellion and to the house of Jacob their sins. For day after day they seek me out; they seem eager to know my ways, as if they were a nation that does what is right and has not forsaken the commands of its God. They ask me for just decisions and seem eager for God to come near them. 'Why have we fasted,' they say, 'and you have not seen it? Why have we humbled ourselves, and you have not noticed?'

Yet on the day of your fasting, you do as you please and exploit all your workers. Your fasting ends in quarreling and strife, and in striking each other with wicked fists. You cannot fast as you do today and expect your voice to be heard on high. Is this the kind of fast I have chosen, only a day for a man to humble himself? Is it only for bowing one's head like a reed and for lying on sackcloth and ashes?

Is that what you call a fast, a day acceptable to the Lord?

Is not this the kind of fasting I have chosen: to loose the chains of injustice and untie the cords of the yoke, to set the oppressed free and break every yoke? Is it not to share your food with the hungry and to provide the poor wanderer with shelter — when you see the naked, to clothe him, and not to turn away from your own flesh and blood? Then your light will break forth like the dawn, and your healing will quickly appear; then your righteousness will go before you, and the glory of the Lord will be your rear guard. Then you will call, and the Lord will answer; you will cry for help, and he will say: Here am I.

If you do away with the yoke of oppression, with the pointing finger and malicious talk, and if you spend yourselves in behalf of the hungry and satisfy the needs of the oppressed, then your light will rise in the darkness, and your night will become like the noonday. The Lord will guide you always; he will satisfy your needs in a sun-scorched land and will strengthen your frame. You will be like a well-watered garden, like a spring whose waters never fail. Your people will rebuild the ancient ruins and will raise up the age-old foundations; you will be called Repairer of Broken Walls, Restorer of Streets with Dwellings.

If you keep your feet from breaking the Sabbath and from doing as you please on my holy day, if you call the Sabbath a delight and the Lord's holy day honorable, and if you honor it by not going your own way and not doing as you please or speaking idle words, then you will find your joy in the Lord, and I will cause you to ride on the heights of the land and to feast on the inheritance of your father Jacob.' The mouth of the Lord has spoken" (Isaiah 58, NIV).

"Formerly, when you did not know God, you were slaves to those who by nature are not gods. But now that you know God — or rather are known by God — how is it that you are turning back to those weak and miserable principles? Do you wish to be enslaved by them all over again? You are observing special days and months and seasons and years! I fear for you, that somehow I have wasted my efforts on you" (Galatians 4:8-11, NIV).

"He replied, 'When evening comes, you say, 'It will be fair weather, for the sky is red,' and in the morning, 'Today it will be stormy, for the sky is red and overcast.' You know how to interpret the

appearance of the sky, but you cannot interpret the signs of the times. A wicked and adulterous generation looks for a miraculous sign, but none will be given it except the sign of Jonah.' Jesus then left them and went away" (Matthew 16:2-4, NIV).

"I rejoice greatly in the Lord that at last you have renewed your concern for me. Indeed, you have been concerned, but you had no opportunity to show it. I am not saying this because I am in need, for I have learned to be content whatever the circumstances. I know what it is to be in need, and I know what it is to have plenty. I have learned the secret of being content in any and every situation, whether well fed or hungry, whether living in plenty or in want. I can do everything through him who gives me strength. Yet it was good of you to share in my troubles. Moreover, as you Philippians know, in the early days of your acquaintance with the gospel, when I set out from Macedonia, not one church shared with me in the matter of giving and receiving, except you only; for even when I was in Thessalonica, you sent me aid again and again when I was in need. Not that I am looking for a gift, but I am looking for what may be credited to your account. I have received full payment and even more; I am amply supplied, now that I have received from Epaphroditus the gifts you

sent. *They are a fragrant offering, an acceptable sacrifice, pleasing to God. And my God will meet all your needs according to his glorious riches in Christ Jesus"* (Philippians 4:10-19, NIV).

Resources I have found helpful about fasting and prayer include: The late Dr. Bill Bright has written a great resource entitled Your Personal Guide to Fasting and Prayer. In it he writes:

> "If you do not already know of the power and importance of fasting, here are some very important facts:
>
> - Fasting was an expected discipline in both the Old and New Testament eras. For example, Moses fasted at least two recorded forty-day periods. Jesus fasted 40 days and reminded His followers to fast, "when you fast," not if you fast.
> - Fasting and prayer can restore the loss of the "first love" for your Lord and result in a more intimate relationship with Christ.
> - Fasting is a biblical way to truly humble yourself in the sight of God (Psalm 35:13; Ezra 8:21). King David said, *"I humble myself through fasting."*

> **Commented [CL20]:** You mention "Resources" here but only list one and then some other details about fasting. Perhaps you could rephrase this line to simply introduce the Excerpt from Bill Bright and then give in another section the FAQ or quick hits about fasting you have below. And I think the chapter questions at the end should be separate than the information about fasting? I think the organization of this chapter needs a bit more attention

- Fasting enables the Holy Spirit to reveal your true spiritual condition, resulting in brokenness, repentance, and a transformed life.
- The Holy Spirit will quicken the Word of God in your heart and His truth will become more meaningful to you!
- Fasting can transform your prayer life into a richer and more personal experience.
- Fasting can result in a dynamic personal revival in your own life--and make you a channel of revival to others.
- Fasting and prayer are the only disciplines that fulfill the requirements of 2 Chronicles 7:14: *"If my people, who are called by my name, will humble themselves and pray and seek my face and turn from their wicked ways, then will I hear from heaven and will forgive their sin and will heal their land."*

If you fast, you will find yourself being humbled as I did. You will discover more time to pray and seek God's face. And as He leads you to recognize and repent of unconfessed sin, you will experience special blessings from God."[xvi]

The Discipline of Fasting

John Wesley wrote, "Some have exalted religious fasting beyond all Scripture and reason; and others have utterly disregarded it."[xvii]

The scriptural definition of fasting:
To abstain from all food, solid or liquid. (Luke 4:2; Daniel 10:3)

Types of Fasting:
Absolute Fast: To abstain from all food and liquids
(Esther 4:16; Deuteronomy 9:9; and 1 Kings 19:8)

Group Fast: To fast with others.
Private Fasting: Time between you as an individual and God

How Often Should We Fast?

How often one should fast is clearly up to the individual, who should be prompted by the Holy Spirit. (Luke 18:12; Zechariah 8:19)

There is no biblical law commanding regular fasting.

Is fasting a commandment?

In his book *Celebration of Discipline*, Richard J. Foster writes, "Matthew 6:16, *'When*

You Fast...' Jesus is making the assumption that we will fast, and is giving instruction on how to do it properly. He talks about fasting in direct relation to prayer and giving."[xviii]

It's been said that "fasting without prayer is nothing more than a diet."

Christ is not saying that you must fast or even *if* you fast. He puts it very simply, *when* you fast. The people of Israel knew about fasting because it was a practice passed down from generation to generation.

What is the purpose of fasting?

Fasting must forever center on God. It must be God-initiated and God-ordained.

Reflection

What did you like about the chapter?

What did you not understand?

What was challenging?

What does this chapter say about people in general?

What did you learn about God in this chapter?

What changes will you make because you read this chapter?

What do you want to share from this chapter?

Chapter 6
Organic living: Living by Design (Physical Body)

> "May God himself, the God of peace, sanctify you through and through. May your whole spirit, soul and body be kept blameless at the coming of our Lord Jesus Christ" (1 Thessalonians 5:23, NIV).

> "God's way and law of fullness is that of organic life. In the Divine order, life produces its own organism, whether it be a vegetable, animal, human or spiritual. This means that everything comes from the inside. Function, order, and fruit issue from this law of life within. It was solely on this principle that what we have in the New Testament came into being. Organized Christianity has entirely reversed this order."[xix]
> - T. Austin-Sparks

Fully functioning body, soul and spirit...

> "Now the LORD God had planted a garden in the east, in Eden; and there he put the man he had formed. 9 And the LORD God made all kinds of trees grow out of the ground — trees that were pleasing to the eye and good for food. In the middle of the garden were the tree of life and the tree of the knowledge of good and evil" (Genesis 2:8-9, NIV).

Jesus said, *"Feed my lambs"* (John 21:15, NIV).

"Let food be thy medicine and medicine thy food." – Hippocrates

I recognize that the term "organic" has become a buzz word that some will hang on to for as long as the buzz lasts. It has, according to the principles of epidemics researched by Malcolm Gladwell, and written about in his book *The Tipping Point*, reached epidemic proportions because it is a "sticky idea."[xx] If you believe in a creator and designer of life, which many of us do, then organic living from my perspective simply means getting back to living by design.

I believe God created us and placed us in a garden for a reason. It is no "coincidence" that the healthiest and longest living people on the planet eat healthy, raw, and live foods. Those with the most disease are those who indulge themselves on the packaged foods that we often eat in the West. Some of these healthy and long living people are now losing their children to disease as they have begun to eat processed packaged diets of the West.[xxi]

When I use the term "organic living" I am talking about removing additives or preservatives in our food that keep us from functioning as purely as possible by design. If we began eating and drinking 75% or more by God's design (without man-made or modified foods) we would feel better, and see a difference in our health quickly. We would also realize long term life-changing benefits!

For example, Kelli and I, and our family started moving toward God's design by removing Aspartame and processed sugar from our diet. We were stunned by the result! I have been very active all my life. But as I reached 40 years of age, it was painful for me to climb out of bed in the mornings. I would have to brave the first painful steps each morning, particularly after a hard game of racquetball the previous day. As the day wore on I could walk in a relatively pain free fashion.

We stopped adding sugar to our food; using sugar-laden condiments on our food; and reduced food that turn to sugar in our bodies. To my total surprise, when I awoke in the mornings, after a day of racquetball, I had no joint pain. I actually felt better at age 48 than I had at 40. I now know that there is a lot of research that says excessive sugar creates inflammation, and reduces our body's ability to fight off disease, particularly cancer.

> **Commented [CL26]:** perhaps we should cite this?

Kelli's story

For almost 15 years my wife Kelli suffered from the symptoms that many hard chargers have experienced called *Fibromyalgia*. She began to see a fantastic internist in terms of empathic listening. He took time to sit and listen to her. However, like most medical doctors, he tried to prescribe a pill for every symptom she had.

It got to a point that Kelli was taking as many as five medications to deal with all of her symptoms, which involved her stomach, her back, fatigue, swollen joints, insomnia, and more. She began to wonder if continuing to see him was worth it both physically and financially.

The questions began to mount:
- Was she feeling any better?
- Was her health improving?
- Why was she experiencing so many secondary symptoms?

- Was this really what the Creator and Designer of our bodies desired for her?

She finally decided to stop taking all the medications. *(Note: This is not something we recommend for anyone. We are not giving medical advice here.)* Kelli discovered that although she did not feel much better, she did not feel any worse either. True health is more than how we feel, but we do need to learn to listen to our bodies.

It wasn't long after this that we discovered a more organic way of living that has further transformed our lives. We had some friends who ran *Maximized Living Chiropractic Care Center*. Kelli decided to give it a try because of their holistic and organic approach. Kelli was desperate for help. They told her that they wanted to try to get to some of the root causes of her illness, rather than deal with symptomatic issues. So we began learning about maximizing the mind, the central nervous system, nutrition, oxygen, and lean muscle; and minimizing toxins.

One of the first toxins Kelli removed from her diet was Aspartame and other artificial sweeteners. Within months of regular chiropractic adjustments, removing additives and preservatives from her food; and eating nothing on the "dirty dozen" list, the symptoms of *Fibromyalgia* completely disappeared.

We were totally blown away by these results. One important note worth mentioning here is that we did this as a family. I told Kelli that if we were going to succeed it must become part of our family's culture and we must do this as a family unit. So I kicked my three or four diet cokes a day habit and really have not looked back since.

I have also seen these same principles at work within God's body the Church. We have many additives and preservatives in the body (God's Church) that has made it sick and dysfunctional. I believe one of the biggest problems with the medical model in our country is that the love of money has overtaken it as a, "root of evil." Many who are a part of the system are there for profit rather than the mission of health and well-being of people. There is absolutely nothing wrong with making a profit; however, there is a problem with loving profit (money); it is the root of all evil. (1 Timothy 6:10)

Reflection

What did you like about the chapter?

What did you not understand?

What was challenging?

What does this chapter say about people in general?

What did you learn about God in this chapter?

What changes will you make because you read this chapter?

What do you want to share from this chapter?

Chapter 7
Organic Living: Living by Design (Soul and Spirit)

"If you make an altar of stones for me, do not build it with dressed stones, for you will defile it if you use a tool on it" (Exodus 20:25, NIV).

"If you use stones to build my altar, use only natural, uncut stones. Do not shape the stones with a tool, for that would make the altar unfit for holy use" (Exodus 20:25-26, NLT).

The same is true when "doing church" becomes big business. I agree with Dallas Willard and Ed Stetzer who say: *"Church in America has become a place where religious goods and services are distributed to Christian consumers."*

Christ's church is actually a living organism that lives and moves and has its being in the Creator. (Acts 17:28)

God created Adam and placed him in the Garden of Eden to tend and care for it. He commanded the him, *"You are free to eat from any tree in the garden; but you must not eat from the tree of the knowledge of good and evil, for when you eat from it you will certainly die"* (Genesis 2:15-17, NIV).

The Lord told Adam he was free to eat from any tree in the garden except the tree of the knowledge of good and evil. There was a *Tree of Life* at the center of the garden, representing the life of Christ who is our Source, our Life. God designed each of us to receive Christ, and then demonstrate our love for Him by our obedience compelled by His goodness. He created us to bear His image.

In the garden, there was nourishment for their bodies and spirits. However, in that first garden, Adam failed. His failure impacted us all. When he was expelled, humankind was expelled from the garden, and separated from the *Tree of Life*—the indwelling Christ.

The good news is that Jesus became flesh, stepped into this world, and passed the garden test! He invites us into the garden again where we can partake, eat and receive.

In another garden, the Garden of Gethsemane, when Jesus faced the serpent and his lies, He cried out to the Father and said, *"Not my will but your will be done."* He then embraced the sacrifice of the cross; rose again the third day; and revealed Himself as the *Tree of Life* in a garden. (Also found in Matt 26:36-46; and Luke 22:39-46.)

The Prayer in the Garden

"Then they came to a place which was named Gethsemane; and He said to His disciples, 'Sit here while I pray.' And He took Peter, James, and John with Him, and He began to be troubled and deeply distressed. Then He said to them, 'My soul is exceedingly sorrowful, even to death. Stay here and watch'" (Mark 14:32-34, NKJV).

"At the place where Jesus was crucified, there was a garden, and in the garden a new tomb, in which no one had ever been laid" (John 19:41, NIV).

Food for the body is temporary, but food for the soul is eternal. When we partake of Christ's life we experience the pleasure of getting intimately acquainted with our Creator-Designer. He created us to connect with Him and others. However, there are always other choices. Just as there is junk food for the body, there is also junk food for the soul and the spirit. It will make you sick!

There is a God-shaped gap in our souls that only He can fill. Yet, some of us search for years trying to fill it with other things. All who have encountered the nourishing life of Christ will testify to the fact that only He can fill that void. I am no different. In my early years I thought, "If I just had this girlfriend, that car, this amount of money, that job, this body, that truck…"— and on and on. However, none of those things did, or could have filled the God-vacancy in my heart. I turned to partying and self-medicating to ease the pain of my life without Christ. Like so many others, I was trying many things to find love, joy, peace, self-control, comfort, and etc. which are only found in Him.

It may surprise you to learn that many have even entered the ministry in an attempt to fill the void in their lives. They enjoy feeling good about helping others, but have never experienced the joy of allowing Christ to fill them, and serving others out of the overflow of His Holy Spirit. This invariably leads to disaster. I am convinced that life is only fully lived (abundant life) when lived according to the Creator's design.

His design is for us to receive our life and nourishment from Christ, the *Tree of Life*, who said: *"I am the Vine, you are the branches; apart from me you can do nothing."* This is not complicated. It is quite simple, though not necessarily easy. I started by saying, "God help. I have made a mess of my life

> **Commented [CL32]:** Scripture reference?

trying to fill it with junk, and doing things my way." With this modest prayer I began an incredible journey pursuing Christ who, I discovered later, had first loved and pursued me.

I began eating from the *Tree of Life* (Christ) when I was 20 years old, and I am grateful to have discovered His nourishing life. I did not come to Christ with the assistance of any man or religious organization. I came to Christ in my bedroom after an extended period of soul searching; following a period of wild and selfish living in pursuit of my own pleasure. At the time I came to Christ, I had spent 18 months stoned, smoking weed (marijuana) daily. I often began the moment I awoke in the morning.

> **Commented [CL33]:** Perhaps you should make a new se here entitled "My Story" like you did Kelli's?

However, that wonderful day I heard God's voice (not audibly, but in my heart) say, "The Bible is the Word of God." I believed it was God's voice, and I responded, "I think I have a Bible somewhere?" Sure enough, I found a New Testament on my bookshelf that I had never opened. I read it from cover to cover in two weeks. Although I did not understand a lot of it, many of the words I read were like healing oil on my wounded soul.

I remember making what I called "My God Box," from a shoe box; then writing thoughts, prayers, and verses on paper; and placing them in that box. I cried out for help, and in faith, I prayed. They weren't "mature prayers," but they were sincere prayers. *"When I was a child, I talked like a child, I thought like a child, I reasoned like a child, when I became a man I put childish ways behind me"* (1 Corinthians 13:11).

God began revealing things to me by His Spirit, and began working mysteriously in my life. Out of my overflow, I begin telling people my story; how God was changing me. I knew something had happened within me. As Paul described, I had become *a new creation.* Oh yes, and I stopped smoking weed immediately.

Of course, for me to grow to spiritual maturity in Christ would take time. I would be learning and unlearning for years to come. However, I was definitely different, and I knew it! I began to attend church services and quickly learned that we don't "go to church," *we are the church.* Even then, somehow I intuitively knew there was something wrong with the church culture. Symptoms of that included too much focus on what one wore; on buildings, programs, and business. I saw, and still see, too little emphasis on the power of God, the indwelling Christ, and Christ-centered community.

I'm glad to say that I did taste some incredible fruit praying and experiencing life with our single adult group. It took me a while to journey through my institutional roots of the south to discover a deeper life of organic living, and I have certainly not yet arrived. Gladly, I am growing, and am still on the journey today. Unfortunately, much of what we (God's people) are, and what we do, is based on American Christian culture and tradition rather than on the apostolic mission of God's kingdom. I will deal with this more later.

I began following Christ in 1986, and three years later started serving as minister of youth in a traditional church (the congregational model). Some great families in that fellowship took me in and taught me the importance of the dinner table. It was also there that I encountered the pain of dysfunctional legalism, and religious tradition. However, in time I found a spiritual father and mother, Charles and Janice Culpepper, who taught me the deeper life in Christ. They introduced me to books by, or about, great Christ-followers of the past like Dawson Trottman, Watchman Nee, C.T.

Studd, Major Ian Thomas, Hudson Taylor, George Mueller, Jim Elliot, Norman Grubb, Corrie Ten Boom, and J.O. Frazier, to name a few. They lived in ways that reflected an understanding of the indwelling Christ, and modeled that for me for which I am forever grateful. For eight years we shared life together and faced the struggles of institutional church life. We transitioned the church from committees to communities; from Sunday school classes to small groups and teams. I grew a lot during those years, and was eventually sent out to plant a new church based on a vision for New Testament community.

In 1997 my wife Kelli and I, along with 11 others we had discipled and shared life with at *Fellowship of Champions*, set out to start a new church. We launched with what we called a 20/20 vision from Acts 20:20 where we see Paul's example of public and house to house ministry. So, we began to meet from house to house during the week in small groups (cell groups). Our plan was to live life together and learn to live the *"one another's"* in the Bible. We were not going to create a bunch of programs. It seemed like a crazy idea at the time. We were the only church in our association of churches (approximately 500 congregations) that did not employ programs. I would tell our people that following Jesus was *our program,* and that we experienced *church* in our cell groups.

The only reason we even held traditional Sunday worship services was that I felt it was a culturally-appropriate way we could attract people and funnel them into a New Testament community where they could experience the *"one another's"* that Christ and Scripture command us to follow. It was a powerful, effective vision, and the start was explosive.

We began with three home groups before we ever conducted the first large Sunday morning celebration service. In January of '98 we started our Sunday services with an incredible minister of music, John Gundersen; and grew rapidly from three to 15 groups in approximately two years, baptizing 20 to 25 new converts each year. I did not like the fact that there was a separation between clergy (we professional ministers) and the laity (the church members).

So, I began to challenge each of our members to become missionaries. We called our home group facilitators, "Community Pastors." I now feel that was a mistake. Why? The illness in the body of Christ created by titles (separating clergy and laity) cannot be cured by handing out more titles. However, it was a great time of learning. Our heart was to capture New Testament community, and in many ways we tasted it.

In 1999 God opened the door for Kelli and me to go to Ethiopia. It was in Ethiopia that God opened my eyes to the various ways I viewed life through the lens of an American rather than as a citizen of the Kingdom of God. I began to see that from Genesis to Revelation God's heart is for all nations, and that He blesses us to be a blessing. I also discovered that I was as effective, if not more so, when I presented Christ and the principles of His Kingdom to cultures other than my own.

This revelation of my cross-cultural effectiveness gave me a desire to function the way God had designed and gifted me, not according to the minister mold society had created for me. God put me through some tests and some deaths to self so I could experience a deeper life in Christ. This meant I would die to myself each day, and learn to live by the indwelling Christ's power. (Galatians 2:20) Basically, I came to a place where the only position I wanted was to see Jesus as Lord of my life, and His church.

I had wrestled as many have, and died to the "get famous for Jesus" attitude that is so pervasive in American Christian culture. I sought a position of leadership in my flesh, but the more I grew in Christ, even that desire began to decrease. This took several years. In about 2009 I remember God speaking to my heart. I was to stop trying to make stuff happen with my own charisma and ability; and start engaging in what I saw Him doing. (John 5:19) This was particularly difficult due to the fact that the Sunday morning worship services (the celebration side of our congregational experience) required leadership that could and would, "make stuff happen."

So, this step of obedience was very difficult. It led me to some amazing places. As a side note: when we step out with this kind of obedience, we should be prepared to be misunderstood. And it's wise to avoid trying to justify or defend our positions. This is an area where it is best to silently obey like Jesus.

As I continued my journey of obedience, I continued to grow, to change, and to see things differently. Many Christians want to put God in "an unchanging doctrine box," which limits their spiritual growth. Doctrine does not produce growth or unity, yet in most Christian circles it is considered the most important issue. It's not that doctrine (truth) does not matter, but that *Truth is a person*. Jesus said of Himself, *"I am the Way, the Truth and the Life"* (John 14:6). God's greatest gift to us is a person not a book.

Therefore, when we have *the Truth* (Christ Jesus) in our lives, He provides the power for us to become like Him. It is Christ-like humility that ultimately protects and provides unity within any gathering of Christ-followers. The organic life of Christ at the center of His *ekklesia* is essential for unity and kingdom effectiveness. This frees us from any need to be propped up by the institutional trappings of by-laws, policies, and procedures, which have very little to do with the advancement of God's kingdom or our being empowered by His Holy Spirit.

(Note: I would like to thank Neil Cole, Frank Viola and Bill Hull for walking through this season with me from a distance as I read their books about multiplying disciples and organic church.)

> The late Dr. A. W. Tozer, preacher and author, is attributed with saying, "If the Holy Spirit was withdrawn from the church today, 95 percent of what we do would go on and no one would know the difference. If the Holy Spirit had been withdrawn from the New Testament church, 95 percent of what they did would stop, and everybody would know the difference."
>
> In his book *Forgotten God,* Francis Chan writes, "Perhaps we're too familiar and comfortable with the current state of the church to feel the weight of the problem. But what if you grew up on a desert island with nothing but the Bible to read? Imagine being rescued after twenty years and then attending a typical evangelical church. Chances are you'd be shocked (for a whole lot of reasons, but that is another story).
>
> Having reading the Scriptures outside the context of contemporary church culture,

you would be convinced that the Holy Spirit is as essential to a believer's existence as air is to staying alive. You would know that the Spirit led the first Christians to do unexplainable things, to live lives that didn't make sense to the culture around them, and ultimately to spread the story of God's grace around the world."[xxii]

Much of what we do is mechanical, not organic. It is therefore not connected to the Divine Energy Source. There is spiritual energy that God produces that affects matter. That's why medicine and mechanisms will never produce holistic healing. It is by having God's Spirit in us, and living by His design (organically) in body, soul and spirit that is the true path to healing.

Interestingly, it was about 2009 when, as I mentioned earlier, Kelli and I met Dr. Mick and Traci Mahan of *The Discover Chiropractic Health Center*, who introduced us to a more holistic way of health. We learned that our bodies were created to heal themselves when they are fully functioning. The problem is that subluxation, like a blockage or choking out of life, keeps us from functioning fully.

Many things can interfere with our physical, spiritual, and emotional health. As we, as a family, began to learn and change our behavior related to health we began to see life from a different perspective. Oswald Chambers said that character growth is a prerequisite for revelation.[xxiii] I like to say, that the application of information leads to transformation. This means that when, motivated by His love, you obey Christ and change your attitudes and behavior your vision for transformation will develop and you'll become Christ-like over time.

Disobedience, as a disease of the soul, interferes with the healing process.

In the natural, there are additives and preservatives that are toxic to our physical bodies. They keep us from functioning in peak performance, the way we were designed to. The separation of the professional clergy and laity is toxic to Christ's body, the church. We won't find that distinction in the New Testament narrative. All of God's children are to be ministers—royal priests.

A focus on secondary doctrines will also rob us of the unity described in Philippians chapter two and Ephesians chapter four. Christ-like humility is the key to our unity as His people. A key difference for we who follow Christ, compared to adherents to other religions, is that we believe God's greatest gift to us is more than a book (teachings); it is a Person. Life, through the power of the Holy Spirit, has been given to us by the Father in His Son. We need not fear diversity. Unity is not synonymous with uniformity. The God of unity is also the God of diversity. As the Godhead is three in one, we can experience the reality of unity in our diversity.

The four "Killer B's", which are banks, buildings, budgets, and boards, have led the church to function more like a business than a body—the bride of Christ, and dwelling of the Holy Spirit. We can build large profitable organizations apart from the power of the Holy Spirit. Much like in the food industry today, a lot of the "church growth industry" focuses on profit and numerical growth ("nickels and noses") rather than spiritual health. Additives and preservatives are largely there to increase profitability and organizational size.

Jesus said His church would be built upon Him. Scripture teaches that the foundational layers are the apostles and prophets. They are the ones who point us to Christ as the

Foundation. Unfortunately, we often opt for profit and numerical growth and utilize the aforementioned Killer B's. Because we have elevated profits over prophets we are not seeing the production of Christ-like disciples and the extension of His kingdom. On the contrary, we are creating consumers who patronize "churches" who provide them with the best religious goods and services. I do recognize that the pursuit of "profits" is sometimes an effort to keep the doors open and the lights on.

For the majority of pastors and churches there is no evil intent to pursue money, it is just the nature of running the church in an incorporated (non-profit) business culture. The tail begins to wag the dog. I have many good friends (some with whom I partner) who lead churches with the Killer B's who have a heart for discipleship and the extension of God's kingdom who certainly are having a greater impact than I.

I do not want to see church buildings torn down in Jesus' name; but I would like to see them used as training centers and sending bases that produce disciples rather than to attract consumers. I am grateful for the example set by those who are doing these very things. I pray that they would be like the Hall of Tyrannus in Acts 19, and that the Gospel will go forth to the uttermost parts of the Earth.

Millions of Americans live in the shadow of churches that have become "consumer Christian centers." Pastors and the mission of God are ruined when consumers simply enjoy the goods and services provided by their local churches. In their book, *God is Back,* John Micklethwait and Adrian Wooldridge describe the state of the American church as having a "Disneyfication" of God, or as being "Christianity Lite – a bland and sanitized faith that is about as dramatic as the average shopping mall."[xxiv]

Believers who think like customers contribute to America's underachieving churches. The damages extend far beyond ineptness at engaging the mission of God. The incessant demands of a consumer congregation cause irreparable damage to those who lead them. Some of the consumer demands are based on pastoral perception too. Many pastors often experience chronic anxiety because they fear their flock.

Jesus Christ was very clear when he stated that we (His followers) are to go and make disciples. Our purpose is to express His life together in a community called the church or *ekklesia*, and there to multiply His life by making disciples. When we focus on loving God, loving people, and making disciples we will see Christ's life expressed through His people organically. When we commit to buildings, staffs, programs, and budgets we embrace additives and preservatives that will ultimately diminish the vitality of the living organism called the church.

The sad thing is that most of us *do church* the way that we are doing it because of our culture. While in other places, where there are no big buildings, budgets, staff and programs the Gospel is multiplying and spreading like we read about in the Book of Acts. Could it be that our cultural way of doing things is robbing us of experiencing God's fruitful multiplication?

God's greatest desire is to see His people live out His eternal purpose. (Ephesians 3:7-12) That means that we are to gather as the body of Christ and express His life. It means that we are to make Christ the head and foundation of our gatherings. No one will hold positions, but each individual will function as a member of the body. This can only be accomplished by the power of God working through people who understand that true life is generated by the indwelling Christ. These are people who will say, "Lord, I can't but you can. You are in us and we choose to allow you to live through us. All life is *'from you, to you and through you!'"* (Romans 11:36) They recognize that envy and strife as a way of life among the members of the body is demonic.

> *"But if you have bitter envy and self-seeking in your hearts, do not boast and lie against the truth. This wisdom does not descend from above, but is earthly, sensual,* demonic. *For where envy and self-seeking exist, confusion and every evil thing are there. But the wisdom that is from above is first pure, then peaceable, gentle, willing to yield, full of mercy and good fruits, without partiality and without hypocrisy. Now the fruit of righteousness is sown in peace by those who make peace"* (James 3:14-18, NKJV).

> *"His intent was that now, through the church, the manifold wisdom of God should be made known to the rulers and authorities in the heavenly realms, according to his eternal purpose which he accomplished in Christ Jesus our Lord. In him and through faith in him we may approach God with freedom and confidence. I ask you, therefore, not to be discouraged because of my sufferings for you, which are your glory"* (Ephesians 3:10-13, NIV).

Organic living involves fully functioning the way God intends. In the fourth chapter of Ephesians, we are told that Jesus has given us equippers who are gifted to help mature the body of Christ. (I think it is very important to note that fully functioning and maturity are ongoing processes of our living dynamic lives, and not a state of perfection.) The word "equip" in Ephesians chapter four refers to a healer or a doctor who helps the body align in such a way that it functions fully.

They help remove all subluxations within the body. Subluxation is a word that refers to interferences that prevent the body from functioning fully. Where there is subluxation, there is disease (dis-ease). When Jesus said that His yoke is easy, He was referring to a divine connection that is free from subluxation so that His disciples could fully function. He was also communicating that the religious leaders of His time where creating "yokes" (yoke meant a way of life) of subluxation (dis-ease). *Sub-* in the word subluxation means below, under or less. *Lux* means light or Divine Light. So a subluxation is where there is less than optimal light or godly energy—Holy Spirit power.

The Bible speaks of five roles or functions. They are the apostle, prophet, evangelist, pastor and teacher. These are mature believers who serve and help the body grow and function. They are servants, who like Jesus remove subluxation from the body of Christ. Jesus calls them greatest in the kingdom because they, like Him, serve to help us walk in the light as He is in the light.

If we could view these five roles as "systems" within the body we would see how important they are for the body's growth and maturity. Unfortunately, we've all but ignored three of these systems--the apostle, the prophet, and the evangelist over the years. However, recently there's been a movement back to what many call "the fivefold ministry." This realignment is going to bring about a greater health in

Christ's body and local gatherings as they learn to operate with these functions.

Jesus came to fill us with His life, His light, and His energy. As we are aligned in mission and expression we will more clearly see and express Jesus Christ. So a gathering of people with Christ as their foundation and head will literally become the hands, the feet, the voice and the total expression of Jesus Christ through the power of His Holy Spirit. Jesus has ascended into heaven and has appointed and anointed men and women as gifts to help align His body so we can function according to His design. Perhaps you are asking, "Okay, what exactly does this look like?"

There are several books that go into this a lot more in depth than I am here. The books *Houses that Change the World* by Wolfgang Simpson, and *Primal Fire* by Neil Cole address what these fivefold ministers look and function like more in-depth.[xxv]

Neil Cole in *Primal Fire* alludes to each of these functions (apostle, prophet, evangelist, shepherd, and teacher) as systems within the human body, each part or equipper representing a different system in our anatomy. He describes the apostolic function like the endocrine or glandular system. This is responsible for dividing what the body needs for proper development, growth, reproduction and mood regulation.

The prophet is like the central nervous system which connects every part of the body to the head and is concerned with making sure the messages from the head reach all parts of the body.

The evangelist's function is like the musculoskeletal system which enables the body to move forward and reach out and touch the world around us. It is the system of motion.

The shepherd functions like the circulatory system which brings oxygen to the body, pumps the blood and keeps everything warm. The teaching functions is like the workings of the digestive system in that it makes sure that the body is well-nourished, separates nourishment and waste, and has the energy and stamina to fulfill its tasks.

I like to say that the apostle provides patterns, foundations, systems and inspiration so that everyone knows that they have a role to play and can *"do all things"* in the power of Christ. When the foundation is right the function is right. The prophet reminds us that we must hear from God, and that His people (His body) need encouragement; to be built up, and sometimes to be comforted. He or she is calling for alignment so that the body may express His life.

The evangelist smiles, inspires us, and challenges us to reach out to others, constantly reminding us that there is a need to move outside of ourselves so that others may know Christ's love. The shepherd is there to encircle everyone (or build circles) and let them know that they are important. Everyone is in need of care, comfort and counsel.

The teacher digs in and discovers details, and distributes them to others; teaching them to teach others so the message will develop deep roots and spread.

All of these gifts help us become more like Christ, the kind of disciples who obey and advance His kingdom. Sadly, there are too few local bodies that experience the influence of these functions working together, organically expressing His life. Again, God wants us to gather as a living organism, His body, a family that produces and reproduces His life.

Interestingly, the gifts of God are lubricated with love. As we maintain our connection with Him, His love will overflow through us to others in an expression of His character, Christ likeness, and mingled with these spiritual gifts will be the fruit of His Spirit.

> "But to each one of us grace was given according to the measure of Christ's gift. Therefore He says: 'When He ascended on high, He led captivity captive, and gave gifts to men.' (Now this, 'He ascended' — what does it mean but that He also first descended into the lower parts of the earth? He who descended is also the One who ascended far above all the heavens, that He might fill all things.) And He Himself gave some to be apostles, some prophets, some evangelists, and some pastors and teachers, for the equipping of the saints for the work of ministry, for the edifying of the body of Christ, till we all come to the unity of the faith and of the knowledge of the Son of God, to a perfect man, to the measure of the stature of the fullness of Christ; that we should no longer be children, tossed to and fro and carried about with every wind of doctrine, by the trickery of men, in the cunning craftiness of deceitful plotting, but, speaking the truth in love, may grow up in all things into Him who is the head — Christ — from whom the whole body, joined and knit together by what every joint supplies, according to the effective working by which every part does its share, causes growth of the body for the edifying of itself in love" (Ephesians 4:7-16, NKJV).

Organic living cannot be accomplished outside of an organic community. The benefits of living in community are significant and have been known to possess healing power:

Malcolm Gladwell, in his book, *The Outliers*, begins with an introduction about the Roseta Mystery. Simply put, the mystery was why people die of old age. That's it. After a great deal of time and research was invested to solve the mystery; it was discovered that the health of the Rosetans was directly connected to the community life in which they lived, and were surrounded by their entire lives.

> "No one was used to thinking about health in terms of community. Wolf and Bruhn had to convince the medical establishment to think about health and heart attacks in an entirely new way: they had to get them to realize that they wouldn't be able to understand why someone was healthy if all they did was think about an individual's personal choices or actions in isolation. They had to look beyond the individual. They had to understand the culture that he or she was a part of and who their friends and family were and what town their families came from. They had to appreciate the idea that the values of the world we inhabit and the people we surround ourselves with have a profound effect on who we are."[xxvi]

However, as healthy as living in community can be, the difficulty of living in community is also a reality. If we are to become like Christ, we too will suffer betrayal by our own Judas'. They are typically someone with whom we are living in close community. The only way the healthy expression of Christ's life in community can be accomplished is through a deep connection to Him—the Vine, the Tree of Life. This expression of life only occurs as individuals abide (cling to, rely on and trust in) in Christ which leads to an overflowing love for one another.

Honestly, dealing with people can be very difficult. I've said for years that "ministry would be great without the people, but it is the people who make it great." All of us are called and appointed to be connected to the body of Christ. When we are connected to His body we will look to Christ in every aspect of our lives. We will see growth in our lives that could never have been accomplished on our own. We all need community. Living in community benefits our physical health, as we challenge one another, build up one another, comfort and encourage one another. (1 Corinthians 14:3)

In addition, we will maintain better physical health as we eat the food God designed for us to eat, and live the way God designed us live. In community we can co-op the procurement of our food, and help feed one another and others who are without, as well. I would love to see Christ communities organized to create gardens of fresh, raw food; and who work together to help feed the poor.

Communities like these could lovingly support one another as they are gathering and going. I'm not talking about big farms; although that would be great. I'm talking about simple organic backyard gardens with fruit and nut trees that can yield food year round in our back yards. An organic community is a holistic approach where we are set apart like it says in 1 Thessalonians 5:23 (spirit, soul, and body).

Organic community provides the friction we need to grow spiritually and become the precious stones built together. It also provides the emotional comfort we need, as well as the divine Truth we need to maintain mental health. In its maturity, living in community is the most beautiful creation upon the earth. After all, it is the bride of Christ in all of her beauty on display to the heavens (Eph. 3:10-11) and the Earth. She is functioning the way God intended!

In addition, she becomes an environment for the reproduction of disciples. Achieving spiritual maturity in the context of community isn't always easy. At times it is painful, difficult, and even gory. In fact, it is impossible! Remember, it is God who makes all things possible. It can be done but only by the power of God's Son! Jesus demonstrated organic community with His disciples and promised to give them the energy (Holy Spirit power) to live it. *"You shall receive power,"* He told them. It's His Holy Spirit power that will reproduce His life around the world.

Note: The "organic community" or church I am referring to is free from the institutional trappings of buildings, budgets, staff, and programs. It can meet virtually anywhere. It is deeply connected to Christ as its Head.

Reflection

What did you like about the chapter?

What did you not understand?

What was challenging?

What does this chapter say about people in general?

What did you learn about God in this chapter?

What changes will you make because you read this chapter?

What do you want to share from this chapter?

Chapter 8
The Environment Matters

"Neither do men pour new wine into old wineskins. If they do, the skins will burst, the wine will run out and the wineskins will be ruined. No, they pour new wine into new wineskins, and both are preserved" (Matthew 9:17, NIV).

God created unique environments in which His creation thrives and displays vitality. Anytime you see something that God has created removed from its environment you will see it lose its vitality, its ability to function by design. For example when you put a lion in a cage or a killer whale in a tank for an extended period of time they begin to lose their instinctive functions. They forget how to hunt, to protect the pride or the pod in that artificial environment. They are no longer free to be who they were created to be.

Of course, in the manufactured environments in zoological gardens, effective caretakers try to emulate aspects of the true environment. Even so, once the animals become institutionalized it is very difficult, and in most cases impossible, to successfully release them back into the wild. They have forgotten or lost the ways of their habitat. Think about it. If God created us to live *in Christ*, then what is the best environment for us to grow to maturity in as His disciples?

The God-approved environment in which we as believers are to live is called the *ekklesia*; referred to in

Scripture as a body, a living organism. It is this transformative environment where we are in Him and He is in us that we are to be native to once we are born again. This environment is a new kingdom God has had on His heart since the beginning of time. This kingdom has a King but it does not have worldly structures like political hierarchies. It is comprised of citizens of Heaven, people who are aliens here, part of a new race that live together in a life-giving community. Love is the evidence of our citizenship.

If we were to ask God, "Of all You created, what to you is the most beautiful thing on Earth?" I suspect He would say, "The most beautiful thing on Earth is the local *ekklesia* functioning as the body or the bride of my Son." The problem is that we have pieced His bride together into sort of a man-made Frankenstein monster. We have allowed our culture and our traditions to dictate what she looks like. The apostolic patterns that were established by Jesus and His original 12 disciples; and by the apostles and prophets that Jesus gave as gifts to His body have been largely forgotten. Some of the most glaring distinctive patterns that have been lost or forgotten are discipleship, community (prophesying over one another), The Lord's Supper as a covenant meal, and recognition of the five-fold ministry gifts God has placed in the church to bring us to maturity.

Paul described in his letter to the Corinthians three foundational tasks that the *ekklesia* of God should fulfill:

- We should make kingdom decisions because we have the mind of Christ.
- We should participate regularly in the Lord's Supper together.

- We should experience body life together, which includes the desire to prophesy over one another. Which he described as building up one another, encouraging one another, and comforting one another.

These three tasks serve as a three-legged throne on which our King Jesus is to sit as He reigns, rules, connects with, and directs His people.

When God's people are rightly connected to Christ as their Head, and are free from man-made toxins and interferences, they will function with a vitality that will produce much fruit from the Vine—The Tree of Life. This is the DNA of God's kingdom that works in and through His body; it is the ONLY environment in which the *Great Commandment* (Matthew 22:37-40); the *Great Commission* (Matthew 28:18-20); and the *Great Expression* (John 15) can be fulfilled.

When the environment we call church is geared towards consumers, we produce consumers. But when the environment is God's vineyard, the Vine will produce fruit for holy wine. Like the prayer Jesus prayed over the wine at Passover, *"Blessed are you, O Lord our God, King of the universe, Creator of the fruit of the vine."* As His followers, our job is to be new wineskins filled with the fruit of the Vine that will satisfy those in the world who thirst for Him.

As we produce true disciples of Christ, not just members who are committed to the vision and values of an organization, we will see our cultures transformed. *Wineskins*: "Wine-", is a symbol of God's Holy Spirit, which is our connection to the Divine and brings love, joy, and peace to our hearts. "-Skins", symbolizes the sacrificial death of Christ that cleanses us and makes it possible for us to be His dwelling place in the earth. We are the vessels who contain this Treasure—Christ's life! (2 Cor. 4:7)

Interestingly, Jesus has given us (His body) apostles and prophets. They are His gifts to help lay a foundation that focuses on Him. The prophet constantly reminds us of our need for the Wine; and the apostle helps us work together by creating simple, reproducible systems (new wine-skins) that help get God's Wine to the ends of the earth.

> *"Consequently, you are no longer foreigners and aliens, but fellow citizens with God's people and members of God's household, built on the foundation of the apostles and prophets, with Christ Jesus himself as the chief cornerstone. In him the whole building is joined together and rises to become a holy temple in the Lord. And in him you too are being built together to become a dwelling in which God lives by his Spirit"* (Ephesians 2:19-22, NIV).

So, the best environment in which to make disciples is the habitat of God, His family, His dwelling, His body, that gathers and goes expressing His life. In this spiritual family children are raised to maturity following Jesus as modeled for them by those who are mature servant equippers. Jesus trained His disciples by example. Here is His process:

- He did the stuff while they watched.
- They assisted Him as He did the stuff.
- Then He assisted, as they did the stuff.
- Then He watched them do the stuff.

It's virtually impossible for this process to be caught in most of our western church models because most consist of a performer or two, while everyone watches. As someone has rightly said, "It's more caught than taught." Our inorganic institutional western model offers little or no vitality.

In Mark 4, Jesus referred to the environment being produce in a field (the world) as having good soil (disciples) that reproduces 30, 60 and 100 fold. The harvest is dependent upon the environment.

Reflection:

Red in the movie, The Shawshank Redemption: "These walls are funny. First you hate 'em; then you get used to 'em. Enough time passes, you get so you depend on them. That's institutionalized."[xxvii]

"Anyone who breaks one of the least of these commandments and teaches others to do the same will be called least in the kingdom of heaven, but whoever practices and teaches these commands will be called great in the kingdom of heaven" (Matthew 5:19-20, NIV).

"I am the true vine; my Father is the gardener. He cuts off every branch of mine that does not produce fruit. And he trims and cleans every branch that produces fruit so that it will produce even more fruit. You are already clean because of the words I have spoken to you. Remain in me, and I will remain in you. A branch cannot produce fruit alone but must remain in the vine. In the same way, you cannot

produce fruit alone but must remain in me. "I am the vine, and you are the branches. If any remain in me and I remain in them, they produce much fruit. But without me they can do nothing" (John 15:1-6, NCV).

"Your kingdom come, your will be done on earth as it is in heaven" (Matthew 6:10, NIV).

"But seek first his kingdom and his righteousness, and all these things will be given to you as well" (Matthew 6:33, NIV).

"Still other seed fell on good soil, where it produced a crop — a hundred, sixty or thirty times what was sown. He who has ears, let him hear" (Matthew 13:8-9, NIV).

"The field is the world, and the good seed stands for the sons of the kingdom. The weeds are the sons of the evil one..." (Matthew 13:38-39, NIV).

"At that time the disciples came to Jesus and asked, "Who is the greatest in the kingdom of heaven?" He called a little child and had him stand among them. And he said: "I tell you the truth, unless you change and become like little children, you will never enter the kingdom of heaven. Therefore, whoever humbles himself like this child is the greatest in the kingdom of heaven" (Matthew 18:1-4, NIV).

"Then the mother of the sons of Zebedee came up to him with her sons, and kneeling before him she asked him for something. And he said to her, "What do you want?" She said to him, "Say that these two sons of mine are to sit, one at your right hand and one at your left, in your kingdom." Jesus answered, "You do not know what you are asking. Are you able to drink the cup that I am to drink?" They said to him, "We are able." He said to them, "You will drink my cup, but to sit at my right hand and at my left is not mine to grant, but it is for those for whom it has been prepared by my Father." And when the ten heard it, they were indignant at the two brothers. But Jesus called them to him and said, "You know that the rulers of the Gentiles lord it over them, and their great ones exercise authority over them. It shall not be so among you. But whoever would be great among you must be your servant, and whoever would be first among you must be your slave, even as the Son of Man came not to be served but to serve, and to give his life as a ransom for many" (Matthew 20:20-28, ESV).

"Jesus replied: "'Love the Lord your God with all your heart and with all your soul and with all your mind.' This is the first and greatest commandment. And the second is like it: 'Love your neighbor as yourself.' All the Law and the Prophets hang on these two commandments" (Matthew 22:37-40, NIV).

"Now as they were eating, Jesus took bread, and after blessing it broke it and gave it to the disciples, and

said, "Take, eat; this is my body." And he took a cup, and when he had given thanks he gave it to them, saying, "Drink of it, all of you, for this is my blood of the covenant, which is poured out for many for the forgiveness of sins. I tell you I will not drink again of this fruit of the vine until that day when I drink it new with you in my Father's kingdom" (Matthew 26:26-29, ESV).

"Then Jesus came to them and said, "All authority in heaven and on earth has been given to me. Therefore go and make disciples of all nations, baptizing them in the name of the Father and of the Son and of the Holy Spirit, and teaching them to obey everything I have commanded you. And surely I am with you always, to the very end of the age" (Matthew 28:18-20, NIV).

"So from now on we regard no one from a worldly point of view. Though we once regarded Christ in this way, we do so no longer. Therefore, if anyone is in Christ, he is a new creation; the old has gone, the new has come! All this is from God, who reconciled us to himself through Christ and gave us the ministry of reconciliation: that God was reconciling the world to himself in Christ, not counting men's sins against them. And he has committed to us the message of reconciliation. We are therefore Christ's ambassadors, as though God were making his appeal through us. We implore you on Christ's behalf: Be reconciled to God. God made him who had no sin to be sin for us, so that in him we might become the *righteousness of God"* (2 Corinthians 5:16-21, NIV).

"But you are a chosen people, a royal priesthood, a holy nation, a people belonging to God, that you may declare the praises of him who called you out of darkness into his wonderful light. Once you were not a people, but now you are the people of God; once you had not received mercy, but now you have received mercy. Dear friends, I urge you, as aliens and strangers in the world, to abstain from sinful desires, which war against your soul. Live such good lives among the pagans that, though they accuse you of doing wrong, they may see your good deeds and glorify God on the day he visits us" (1 Peter 2:9-12, NIV).

Reflection

What did you like about the chapter?

What did you not understand?

What was challenging?

What does this chapter say about people in general?

What did you learn about God in this chapter?

What changes will you make because you read this chapter?

What do you want to share from this chapter?

Chapter 9
The Blights (Dis-eases) of Organic Life

The definition of the word *blight*, from Webster's Dictionary: *A disease or injury of plants marked by the formation of lesions, withering, and death of parts (as leaves and tubers): an organism (as an insect or a fungus) that causes blight: something that frustrates plans or hopes: something that impairs or destroys: a deteriorated condition <urban blight>*xxviii

"Take my yoke upon you and learn from me, for I am gentle and humble in heart, and you will find rest for your souls. For my yoke is easy and my burden is light" (Matthew 11:29-30, NIV).

When we connect to Christ, we receive a life source that makes the impossible, possible. Producing spiritual fruit, which is supernatural, becomes natural. This is because our connectedness to Christ is how God designed and intended us to live. You'll remember that He said, *"My yoke* (His way of life) *is easy* (not burdensome)." Why? It's easy and becomes second nature to us because it's His nature! He does it in and through us. Therefore, we can be *dis-ease* free. Even life's storms are designed for us to connect more deeply to *"the Way, the Truth and the Life."* In this world we *will* face troubles and disease. But we can take heart knowing that He has overcome the world. This, His promise, is for both *now* and *later*.

Commented [CL50]: Scripture Reference?

I recognize that we all must come to grips with living in a fallen world. Stuff happens! However, we should not overlook the fact that we sometimes reap from a way of life that we have sowed. There are diseases that we bring on ourselves (spirit, soul, and body) because we opted to choose our way over His.

> *"Do not be deceived: God cannot be mocked. A man reaps what he sows. The one who sows to please his sinful nature, from that nature will reap destruction; the one who sows to please the Spirit, from the Spirit will reap eternal life. Let us not become weary in doing good, for at the proper time we will reap a harvest if we do not give up. Therefore, as we have opportunity, let us do good to all people, especially to those who belong to the family of believers"* (Galatians 6:7-10, NIV).

The dangers of *idealism* and *perfectionism*

As members of organic communities there are certain dangers of which we should be aware. One of the greatest destroyers of community life is one's idealistic focus on perfectionism. When I was a younger Christian I struggled with this. My expectations for myself and others resulted in a lot of frustration and conflict. I would even attack people who did not see, or measure up to my idealistic view of things. God's eternal purpose, which is to *make us one as He and the Father are one*; and for His life to be expressed through our unity in community, is destroyed by these workings of the flesh. Never forget, our natural minds are part of our fallenness.

Perfectionism is the fruit of legalism. Striving to please God on our own does not extend the grace necessary to maintain healthy relationships. It also assumes that our singular view of God, who reveals Himself in multi-faceted brilliance, is 100% accurate. In other words, when we do this we play God.

When five people describe the same diamond, they will describe it as they see it from their perspective and the light they are given. One will see the color yellow; another blue; and the third will see green, etc.

The apostle Paul dealt with this in the first century. The Judaizers, who were the perfectionists of his day, pursued him from one town to another persecuting him, and trying to destroy the organic spiritual communities that were expressing Christ's life. They took particular joy in attacking non-Jewish (Gentile) Christ-followers. They persecuted them because they were not "of the circumcision" (meaning, not of Jewish descent), and because they ate unclean food according to the Old Testament law. They judged others based on their traditions and customs. They elevated their belief that every Christian should eat according to the law above knowing, and being in relationship with God. They failed to see that even the act of their eating physical food was symbolic of their feeding on the real source of eternal life, which is Christ Himself.

In addition, in Paul's day we read of the problem of people offering food, whether meat, vegetables or grains, as offerings to pagan gods—idols! For this reason, a lot of scriptures address the issue of food. (1 Corinthians 10) No one's nutritional plan makes them right with God. Every Christ-follower is free to eat whatever he or she desires, and nothing is considered unclean that is received with thanksgiving.

This is made perfectly clear in Scripture. Jesus made it very clear to His original twelve disciples, as well. We see this in the story of Peter and Cornelius, where Peter experienced his noonday rooftop vision of a sheet coming down out of heaven with animals on it. God wanted to make sure that Peter (and us) understood that food does not make us righteous. (Mark 7:1-23; Acts 10) *Christ plus nothing is our righteousness!* However, this is not to say that a proper diet doesn't offer benefits. As Paul said, we are permitted to partake of any food, but not every food is beneficial for us.

Therefore, Christ-followers are free to eat donuts, drink Diet Coke's, and ingest all kinds of horrible foods. They are also free to smoke cigarettes. Smoking a cigarette will not send you to hell; it just makes you smell like you've been there. Eating donuts and drinking Diet Cokes don't send you to hell either. It may just shorten your trip to heaven!

It's always seemed silly to me that Christ-followers who consume tons of harmful toxins into their bodies through improper diets, when they come to death's door as a result of those toxins will say, "It must be God's time." The same person would look down upon someone who drank arsenic to commit suicide. All the while they are slowly committing suicide, consuming one toxin after another, allowing diseases to spread and to prevent their systems from functioning properly. Like my father said after he developed diabetes, "I have been committing suicide with a fork."

So we have this incredible tension in organic communities. On one hand we need to allow people the freedom to choose what they do. While on the other hand, we need to challenge them to live organically according to God's design. This includes eating good food and making good choices. We care about people. We want them to live long holistically healthy lives, and reach their kingdom potential. We receive and take seriously Paul's prayer challenge to be set apart spirit, soul, and body. (1 Thessalonians 5:23)

> "Everything is permissible"-but not everything is beneficial. "Everything is permissible"-but not everything is constructive. Nobody should seek his own good, but the good of others. Eat anything sold in the meat market without raising questions of conscience, for, "The earth is the Lord's, and everything in it" (1 Corinthians 10:23-26, NIV).

> "May God himself, the God of peace, sanctify you through and through. May your whole spirit, soul and body be kept blameless at the coming of our Lord Jesus Christ. The one who calls you is faithful and he will do it" (1 Thessalonians 5:23-24, NIV).

> "Therefore do not let anyone judge you by what you eat or drink, or with regard to a religious festival, a New Moon celebration or a Sabbath day. These are a shadow of the things that were to come; the reality, however, is found in Christ" (Colossians 2:16, 17 NIV).

According to Dietrich Bonhoeffer, "Every human idealized image that is brought into the Christian community is a hindrance to genuine community and must be broken up so that genuine community can survive. Those who love their dream of a Christian community more than the Christian community itself become destroyers of that Christian community even though their personal intentions may be ever so honest, earnest, and sacrificial…

"Those who dream of this idealized community demand that it be fulfilled by God, by others, and by themselves. They enter the community of Christians with their demands, set up their own law, and judge one another and even God accordingly…

"Because God already has laid the only foundation of our community, because God has united us in one body with other Christians in Jesus Christ long before we entered into common life with them, we enter into that life together with other Christians, not as those who make demands, but as those who thankfully receive. We thank God for what God has done for us. We thank God for giving us other Christians who live by God's call, forgiveness, and promise. We do not complain about what God does not give us; rather we are thankful for what God does give us daily."[xxix]

In his book, *The Reason for God*, Tim Keller wrote, "If you center your life and identity on a 'noble cause', you will divide the world into 'good' and 'bad' and demonize your opponents. Ironically, you will be controlled by your enemies. Without them, you have no purpose."[xxx]

Failure to understand the *transformation process*

Closely related to the danger of idealism is a poor understanding of *process*. We must realize and remember that people are *in process*. None of us have arrived. That being said, we need to have a *preferred future* (vision) that we are moving toward. That's why we must grow in grace and truth. God's grace and truth, over time, moves us toward His vision. That is how we grow spiritually.

When we reject people because they have "yet to arrive;" and we fail to accept the fact that they are *in process*, we drive them away rather than influence them toward the vision. If we understand that process is about clearly communicating a vision of a preferred future, while wisely discerning our current reality, we create the tension necessary to move us courageously forward in the power of God's Spirit. When we can clearly see the vision and our current reality, we can discern the vision path which will get us from where we are to where we want to be!

This process of transformation can and will happen if we will put on the mind of Christ and allow His wisdom to guide us. Some will want to use God's grace to eliminate the truth of an ideal or preferred future. Then they wonder why they have not changed. Don't let that be you! Engage the process of transformation. *The pain is worth the gain!*

> *"The Word became flesh and made his dwelling among us. We have seen his glory, the glory of the One and Only, who came from the Father, full of grace and truth. John testifies concerning him. He cries out, saying, "This was he of whom I said, 'He who comes after me has surpassed me because he was before me.'" From the fullness of his grace we have*

all received one blessing after another. For the law was given through Moses; grace and truth came through Jesus Christ" (John 1:14-18, NIV; emphasis mine).

"...that has come to you. All over the world this gospel is bearing fruit and growing, just as it has been doing among you since the day you heard it and understood God's grace in all its truth" (Colossians 1:6, NIV; emphasis mine).

"...as free, yet not using liberty as a cloak for vice, but as bondservants of God" (1 Peter 2:16, NKJV).

"For you are free, yet you are God's slaves, so don't use your freedom as an excuse to do evil" (1 Peter 2:16-17, NLT).

Watch out for *Koinonitis*

There is another dangerous toxin in the body of Christ. "Koinonitis" is a disease that makes the body love the fellowship of community more than Christ Himself. *Koinonia*, the Greek word for fellowship, which can be a wonderful expression of Christ's life. It is an inward focused care for, and love for one another in the family of God (the body of Christ). It was the fellowship (*koinonia*) of the early Christian church that set them apart, and made them attractive to those who observed them from the outside.

However, if our only focus is to care for one another, without reaching out to others, we become a "Dead Sea" (having only inlets and no outlets causes oversaturation which becomes harmful to life), and Koinonitis sets in. This is one reason that we need the influence of apostles and evangelist in the body. They challenge us beyond shallow praying focused on "us four and no more." They keep us from becoming what some call, "the frozen chosen."

There are few spiritual conditions sadder than to see a gathering of Christians who remain focused on the fold, and never follow Jesus the Good Shepherd into the fields. (John 10) At this point they can no longer be called Christ-followers. These unhealthy folks may be fans of Jesus, but they are certainly not followers. Being a fan costs nothing and produces nothing.

> *"They devoted themselves to the apostles' teaching and to the fellowship, to the breaking of bread and to prayer"* (Acts 2:42-43, NIV).

Beware of the dreaded *Expertitis*

In addition to Koinonitis, there is *Expertitis*. This disease occurs when we depend on experts to do things that every member of the body is capable of, and God has said every member of the body should do. Expertitis kills the participatory body life in a gathering of people. They come and sit, rather than learn from and ministering in the power of the Holy Spirit. When there is an "expert" or a group appointed "Bible answer man or woman," everyone has a tendency to turn their heads towards the expert, and expect them to provide answers to all of the questions.

This sometimes feeds the ego of the expert, as well as the dependency of the group on the expert; rather than on Christ and the Holy Spirit. I'm certainly not suggesting that we remove elders, gifted teachers, or other mature people from our groups. They are there to provide guidance, and to constantly point others in the group to Christ and the Holy Spirit.

Expertitis is when an unhealthy codependency develops where teachers (or experts) intentionally or inadvertently create a dependency of others on themselves, rather than to encourage others to depend on Christ. A misguided expert will tend to bask in the accolades, approval, and attention they receive from the group. As the Apostle Paul wrote:

> *"Now about food sacrificed to idols: We know that we all possess knowledge.* Knowledge puffs up, but love builds up. *The man who thinks he knows something does not yet know as he ought to know. But the man who loves God is known by God"* (1 Corinthians 8:1-3, NIV; emphasis mine).

God desires to see His local body express His life to the world around them. When the body is healthy, disease free, and growing to maturity, we will see a loving vertical connection with God; and a horizontal love connection with one another—including those who are not yet part of the body. The spiritual and relational vitality drawn from these connections will cause others to take note that something is radically different with these people. In addition, they will reproduce followers who will also have the opportunity to mature, and express His life. This is God's eternal purpose found in Ephesians 3:10-11. The requirements are a vision, and a preferred future for an expression that includes the mission of Christ.

The diseases I've mentioned can and will keep us from the mission of making disciples. We must guard against them if we are to fully express His life! Organic mission is about a connection that leads to an expression of His life. This happens when we discover who we are, and live out the mission of making disciples.

When we are motivated by love, obedience is an expression of who we are rather than a religious duty we perform. Faith and works become functions of who we are, and are expressed in our body of Christ gatherings. When this connection happens, others encounter Christ as His people are gathering and going. Not all unbelievers will respond; but to some, this encounter will have the sweet fragrance of life they will be in awe that "God is among you." (1 Corinthians 14:25; 2 Corinthians 2:14-16)

Reflection

What did you like about the chapter?

What did you not understand?

What was challenging?

What does this chapter say about people in general?

What did you learn about God in this chapter?

What changes will you make because you read this chapter?

What do you want to share from this chapter?

Chapter 10
Organic Mission The Vision, the Mission and the Expression

Christians often describe their going somewhere, or doing something for God as being "on mission" for Christ. However, I'm not certain that going somewhere and/or doing something for Christ is actually following Christ.

On the other hand, in our attempts to do things for God some good things can result. We sometimes discover who we are, our weaknesses, and the need for our total dependence upon God. We learn that we can't, but He can. Saul of Tarsus was an example of this. He was on his way to do something for God. He was religiously going to persecute and kill some of the people of The Way. While riding horseback to Damascus, blind to the plan God had for him to fulfill, his eyes were opened to the light of who he was created to be. Over a process of time and experience he discovered that God had designed him to be "an Apostle to the Gentiles."

> **Commented [CL58]:** Scripture reference for Paul's conversion and this quote?

Jesus, on the other hand, knew *exactly* who He was. In the eighth chapter of John, He said: *"I know who I am (where I am from) and I know where I'm going."* He was, and is, the Word who *"became flesh and dwelt among us."* (John 1:14) The things Christ did flowed from who He was. Wherever Jesus was physically, He brought with Him his connection to the Father. He was the ultimate model and example of what it means to be a *human being,* and not merely *a human doing.*

Jesus' mission in life was to be who God sent Him to be. He had no sin nature because He was, at that time, "the only begotten son" of the Father, "the first-born among many brethren." He knew who He was from childhood. At age twelve He told His parents, *"I am about my Father's business."* He did not have to put off His sin nature and put on the Father's clothing. *"He was, and is, and is to come."* So wherever Jesus went He was in the Father, and the Father was in Him, working through Him.

He loved, forgave, healed, and proclaimed the good news of the kingdom to the people. That was who He was!

As a result of His sacrificial death, burial, and resurrection, Christ made it possible for you and me to become who God has designed us to be. Because of Jesus, we can know our Creator as "Father." The more risks we take to step out, take His hand, and follow Him, the more we discover who we really are. With Him indwelling our lives, we take Him with us everywhere. Where we are, He is. As we encounter dark places, being who He has designed us to be, we can function as salt and light. As we are filled with His Spirit, we are able to experience and express His love, joy, peace, patience, gentleness, goodness, meekness, self-control, and faith. It is why He created us. A thirsty world needs living water. The Living Water lives in us. As we love God with all our heart, mind, soul, and strength we discover a love for ourselves that frees us to be who we actually are, and to love others as God loves them.

In Jesus, I am free to be the me that God has created me to be. However, there is a catch. The way I discover my being is in doing. His mission matters, but we also need His vision to see how to effectively express His life.

To have our eyes opened to the reality of Christ (Vision) and His kingdom requires a revelation of God's Spirit. The entire Old Testament is leading and pleading for us to see the need for a savior, a divine King, who is the exact representation of who God is, in the flesh, as a man. Jesus is that King. He came to offer us a new covenant. Jesus made possible a new way of life in the Spirit for us. This new way of life always existed, for it is eternal. But sadly too often, we Western Christians embrace Old Testament models and methods that rob us of New Testament revelation, mission and expression. Like those in the Old Testament, we want God to give us a King who is one of us, broken, fallen and incapable of leading us to where the Father wants us to go. We want to follow human leadership rather than divine leadership.

We treat the Old Testament, which was only a foreshadowing of the things to come, as if it is the ultimate reality. The ultimate reality is Jesus Christ. He is the revelation, and the exact representation of God, in human flesh! (Hebrews 1:3) Jesus Christ revealed Himself to us so we could connect to Him in a body that functions as a Tree of Life. He is the Vine and we are the branches. He is the Source of everything we need. He is the Tree of Life! Adam failed in a garden; Jesus did not. He has taken us back to the garden, and has restored all that Adam lost.

Before his notable fall into sin, the first Adam birthed a covenant community from His side--Eve, his beautiful bride. It was a picture of the second Adam (Christ) who birthed a bride from His side at Calvary. He made it possible for local bodies of Christ-followers to be His expressions on Earth until all is redeemed and restored. With Him as the Head, and when we gather with a Christ-centered community of people who are committed to the revelation, mission and expression of Christ's life, we have biblical *ekklesia*—church.

Toward the Reality of the Church

Frank Viola writes in his book, *From Eternity to Here*, "To put it candidly, you will never have an authentic experience of the body of Christ unless your foundation is blindly and singularly Jesus Christ. Authentic church life is born when a group of people are intoxicated with the glorious unveiling of the Lord.

The chief task of a Christian leader, therefore, is to present a Christ to God's people that they have never known, dreamed, or imagined--a breathtaking Christ whom they can know intimately and love passionately. The calling of every Christian is to build the ekklesia upon an overmastering revelation of the Son of God; a revelation that burns in the fiber of his or her being; and leaves God's people breathless, overwhelmed, and awash in the glories of Jesus.

From God's standpoint, the church's center of gravity is Jesus Christ.

To the bride, Christ is the foundation, the cornerstone, and the capstone.

To the body, Christ is the Head.

To the family, Christ is the first born.

When the church is centered on the ultimacy of Christ, it no longer chases Christian "things" or "its." Knowing Christ, exploring Him, encountering Him, honoring Him, loving Him, and expressing Him becomes the church's governing pursuit.

Rightly conceived, the church is a local group of people who have immersed and saturated with the magnificent vision of Jesus Christ and who are discovering how to take Him as their All together and bring Him to the world. This discovery lies at the heart of deep ecclesiology."[xxxi]

In their book, *House Church*, Brian Anderson and Steve Aterkerson write, *"Why do you suppose that Jesus chose the word church to describe His followers? 'Church' is the English translation of the original Greek term ekklesia. Outside the context of the New Testament, ekklesia was a secular word that carried strong political connotations. There were other Greek words Jesus could have used to describe His followers and their gatherings, words that carried religious and non-political connotations…*

Webster's New Collegiate Dictionary states that the English word church can be used to refer to either a meeting of God's people or to the special building in which they meet. In contrast, the Greek word ekklesia never refers to a building or a place of worship, and it can refer to much more than just a meeting, assembly or gathering. Our understanding of God's church will be much impoverished if we fail to factor in the dynamics of the original Greek word used by Jesus. With so much emphasis today on the separation of church and state, the last thing we associate church with is government. Yet, this is exactly the original meaning of ekklesia.

> *During the time of Jesus, the word ekklesia was used almost without exception to refer to a political assembly that was regularly convened for the purpose of making decisions. According to Thayer's lexicon it was 'an assembly of people convened at the public place of council for the purpose of deliberation.' Bauer's lexicon defines ekklesia as an 'assembly of a regularly summoned political body.'"*[xxxii]

We are citizens of an eternal city, a new race of kingdom people. We should gather together as His church (*ekklesia*) to make kingdom decisions. The elders among us should help us make these good decisions because they have the most experience and tend to be wisest in His kingdom ways.

When the Head (Christ) is properly aligned with the body (His people) we reach maximized functionality. When the body is not properly functioning there is some kind of interference. There are many different things that can interfere in our physical bodies and prevent them from reaching their maximum capacity. The same is true in Christ's body (*ekklesia*).

Our lead Apostle Jesus laid the foundation with His life and teaching for future apostles and His apostolic mission. In John 15 He uses the imagery of a Vine and branches to communicate the organic expression of His life in us. Unfortunately, most bottlenecks are the result of leaders who desire to control people for selfish gain, and profit, rather than equip them for their God-designed ministries.

The Great Commission is for us to go and multiply disciples so that a Tree of Life is planted in every city, village, and among every ethnic group (pocket of people) to the ends of the Earth. (John 15; Matthew 28:18-20; and Ephesians 3:7-11)

When the body gathers for body life expression there is open participation. Anyone can have a word, a song, a gift or talent to share with the others.

The focus is to remain on exalting Christ alone, not someone's talent or personality. He will certainly use personalities and talents as we surrender them to God and focus on Him. There is order in the service, but no "Order of Service."

Leadership is also different. A leader's role is to listen and facilitate participation among the members. There will often be an "awe" encountered by those participating as they hear Christ's word for His body—His church. I often describe this sort of gathering as a beautiful mess.

It is a mystery, the mystery of *"Christ in you, the only hope of revealing the characteristics and attributes of God"* (His glory).

> *"But everyone who prophesies speaks to men for their strengthening, encouragement and comfort"* (1 Corinthians 14:3-4, NIV).

> *"So it is with you. Since you are eager to have spiritual gifts, try to excel in gifts that build up the church"* (1 Corinthians 14:12, NIV).

> *"But if an unbeliever or someone who does not understand comes in while everybody is prophesying, he will be convinced by all that he is a sinner and will be judged by all, and the secrets of his heart will be laid bare. So he will fall down and*

worship God, exclaiming, 'God is really among you!' What then shall we say, brothers? When you come together, everyone has a hymn, or a word of instruction, a revelation, a tongue or an interpretation. All of these must be done for the strengthening of the church" (1 Corinthians 14:24-27, NIV).

"Two or three prophets should speak, and the others should weigh carefully what is said. And if a revelation comes to someone who is sitting down, the first speaker should stop. For you can all prophesy in turn so that everyone may be instructed and encouraged. The spirits of prophets are subject to the control of prophets. For God is not a God of disorder but of peace"
(1 Corinthians 14:29-33, NIV).

"To them God has chosen to make known among the Gentiles the glorious riches of this mystery, which is Christ in you, the hope of glory" (Colossians 1:27, NIV).

With each obedient step we become more like Christ, as individuals, and as a community. Further revelation comes as we obey Him. The Holy Spirit fills and reveals the Life of Christ to those who are obedient. As it has been said, "Light is given where light is received." As our character grows, so does our vision of Jesus. That is what it means to magnify the Lord. As a result we become increasingly more like Christ. His supremacy holds everything together and grows us into the bride or body He desires.

A simple way to put this is that we are to be a family who loves God, loves people and makes disciples, who will also make disciples. This is a simple message, but it is not easy; in fact it is impossible. The only way it can be done is in the power of the Holy Spirit.

As each member of a local expression commits to Christ and His mission of disciple making, as an individual in community, a multiplication of disciples takes place that leads to spiritual maturity. The maturity of the group will express itself through body life that includes the equipping ministry of the five-fold gifts (Ephesians 4:11-16).

In addition, groups like these that are on mission and growing toward spiritual maturity, will reproduce over and over again transforming entire people groups! This is the heart of apostolic mission. The sad thing is that in Western culture our institutionalism interferes with and often prevents organic expression. We have to have by-laws, boards, constitutions, and attend meeting-after-meeting; all of which have very little to do with the mission and expression of God's life through us—the body of Christ.

A mature reproducing body understands the power of being filled with the Holy Spirit. They pray over their *oikos* (Greek word connoting one's relational network) and look for opportunities and the persons of peace with whom they can share their story, and His. As people come to know Christ they are trained to obey Him immediately and to train others to do likewise. The training is simple and reproducible, and as disciples are multiplied, new groups are formed to express His Life, and to repeat the process again and again (reproduction).

The mission is to take the seeds of the Tree of Life into the world, spread them, and let it take root, grow, mature, and express His life. Jesus told a story in Mark chapter 4 and Matthew 13 about the sower and the seed. He said there is something about this story that helps us understand all of His stories. (Mark 4:13) He cast a vision and the vision is that a seed can become a tree, and that tree can become a forest. The gospel is so much more than being forgiven, and then being good until you die.

The gospel is a story, *the greatest story ever told*, about a King and His kingdom. It's about being servant warriors in a battle to advance His kingdom until the day He comes to reign. There is darkness, danger, and adventure. But the King makes it worth the risk. There is no greater treasure than the DNA of the kingdom, which is ours to share as His vessels. So, if I show you a seed, what do you see? Do you see a single seed; or can you see the forest?

> "Sam: It's like in the great stories, Mr. Frodo. The ones that really mattered. Full of darkness and danger they were. And sometimes you didn't want to know the end... because how could the end be happy? How could the world go back to the way it was when so much bad had happened? But in the end, it's only a passing thing... this shadow. Even darkness must pass.
>
> "Sam: I wonder if we'll ever be put into songs or tales.
> Frodo: [turns around] What?
> Sam: I wonder if people will ever say, 'Let's hear about Frodo and the Ring.' And they'll say 'Yes, that's one of my favorite stories. Frodo was really

courageous, wasn't he, Dad?' 'Yes, my boy, the most famousest of hobbits. And that's saying a lot.'
Frodo: [continue walking] You've left out one of the chief characters - Samwise the Brave. I want to hear more about Sam. [stops and turns to Sam]
Frodo: Frodo wouldn't have got far without Sam.
Sam: Now Mr. Frodo, you shouldn't make fun; I was being serious.
Frodo: So was I. [they continue to walk]
Sam: Samwise the Brave..."[xxxiii]

In closing, there will come a time when participants in organic living and organic community will no longer be limited to people like me, who long for a purer and simpler expression of body life. Even in America many Christians will be forced underground, to live in secretive organic communities. We are already seeing the loss of our liberty, and a wave of governmental control over many aspects of our lives. The government will seek more and more control over religious institutions for taxation as the nation's economy sinks, and its debt rises.

In some cases, churches will be forced to embrace policies and procedures that go against their biblical values. I have purposely avoided using gloom and doom prognostications, or fear to motivate people to move towards the principles I share in this book. Instead, my prayer is that people will choose organic living based on their personal conviction, seeing that it is a better way of life as a disciple of Christ. However, to prepare for a future national collapse is certainly an additional valid argument to challenge us to move towards this biblical way of life.

Those who are free from the institutional trappings the church has embraced for centuries will be able to more effectively take the church underground. When this happens we will see a spreading, moving, transforming body of Christ, which rapidly reproduces. The beautiful bride of Christ is in preparation for the marriage supper of the Lamb. In the end we will see the image of God's eternal purpose, where all rivers flow to the Tree of Life that produces fruit through the original twelve to all nations!

> "Then the angel showed me the river of the water of life, as clear as crystal, flowing from the throne of God and of the Lamb down the middle of the great street of the city. On each side of the river stood the tree of life, bearing twelve crops of fruit, yielding its fruit every month. And the leaves of the tree are for the healing of the nations. No longer will there be any curse. The throne of God and of the Lamb will be in the city, and his servants will serve him. They will see his face, and his name will be on their foreheads. There will be no more night. They will not need the light of a lamp or the light of the sun, for the Lord God will give them light. And they will reign for ever and ever" (Revelation 22:1-5, NIV).

Reflection

What did you like about the chapter?

What did you not understand?

What was challenging?

What does this chapter say about people in general?

What did you learn about God in this chapter?

What changes will you make because you read this chapter?

What do you want to share from this chapter?

Acknowledgements

I acknowledge and thank my Lord Jesus Christ, the Tree of Life, who is my Source and Sustainer. I write this with fear and trembling knowing that I am a broken man who is in process. However, His perfect love cast out fear. I pray that you will see more of Him in this writing.

I thank you Mom, Dad, Bobby, Theresa, Kelli, Rachel, Candace and Besufekad, (Berhanu my brother from another mother) for your love and support.

Much thanks to Charles and Janice Culpepper for mentoring, modeling and teaching me about the indwelling Christ. I thank the fellowships where I have learned so much on this journey: *The Fellowship of Champions* formally known as *North Champions Baptist Church*; *Crossroads Community Church*; *Church Multiplication Associates*; and the *M4network*.

I am grateful to the *Leaders Edge Community* and *Union Baptist Association* for your boldness to think outside the box; and for *Discover Chiropractic Health Center* for your holistic approach to helping people live out the mission. To those authors on this topic whose pens preceded mine; who mentored and affirmed me from a distance: Dawson Trotman, Ralph Neighbour, Bill Hull, Neil Cole, and Frank Viola.

I thank Tre9 and the *Disciple the Street* soldiers, Lindsay Cofield, Sally Hinzie, Carol Davis, the McCalls, and my *M4* partners. Thank you for being bold enough to live out these principles with me and for providing a safe, yet radical, place for us to learn together.

Thanks to the *Cypress Organic Church* who has expressed His life so clearly, and who have also provided me with editorial advice.

I thank my second home where I have Habesha and Ferenge family in the land that has taught me so much. Ethiopia – I love you!

And finally, I thank Eddie Smith and the *Worldwide Publishing Group* for their support and expertise.

Endorsements

"People do what they value. This is a great tool to understand the functional values that God wants for all of us. You will be blessed by the parallels of our physical function and how we function as a body of Christ. A healthier you is a more effective follower of Christ!"

--**Dr. Mick Mahan**, *Discover Chiropractic Health Center*

"I have had the pleasure and honor of knowing Guy for approximately 14 years. The power that emanates from the pages of this book is the incredible congruity between the man and the message. Having been in his home many times I

can tell you this material is not a theoretical postulation of truth for him, but a lifestyle that has borne fruit for many. In the words of the great theologian, Judge Rienholdt, spoken in *Fast Times at Ridgemont High*, "learn it, know it, live it!"
--**Mark Lecrone,** *Kingdom Professional, Philosopher, Pastor, Prophet, Elder*

"What an encouragement this book is to get back to living the way our Father has intended all along! Our nation is in real trouble, but there is still time to turn it around. Whether you're a parent, grandparent, wife, husband or mentor; family meals and deep communication are need to be part of our lives on a **very regular** basis. This book contains the tools to reestablish godly living so that we can experience the abundant life God offers us! Guy Caskey has the solution to a real problem in our culture today. It's time to implement it. When we do, we will see the real fruit of our labor!
--**Peggi Merkey,** founder of *Can You Hear Me Now, evangelist and passionate youth advocate*

"Guy Caskey has been catalyst in my life to not only share the gospel with the multitudes, but to take on the responsibility to disciple them. Prior to my relationship with Guy, my focus was primarily evangelism. Now that I am a part of the growing M4 Network, I have a much greater call and a strategic focus on how to train disciples to train disciples. I believe both our physical and spiritual health coincide in this book therefore making us more effective Christ-followers."

--**Bobby Tre9 Herring**, Christian rapper, Founder of *Eyes on Me, Inc.*, urban missionary, evangelist, and apostle.

Discovery Questions
1) What did you like about the chapter?
2) What did you not understand?
3) What was challenging?
4) What does this chapter say about people in general?
5) What did you learn about God in this chapter?
6) What changes will you make because you read this chapter?
7) What do you want to share from this chapter?

NOTES
Introduction
[i] Francis, Tina. "My C-Word: An Introduction." A Deeper Story. April 10, 2013. Accessed January 5, 2015. http://deeperstory.com/my-c-word-an-introduction/.

Chapter 1
[ii] *The Matrix*. Warner Bros. Pictures, 2001. Film.
[iii] *American Top 40*. Watermark Inc., 1970. Radio Series.
[iv] Cloud, John. "Why Your DNA Isn't Your Destiny." *Time Magazine*, January 6, 2010.
[v] The Lord of the Rings: The Fellowship of the Ring. New Line Home Entertainment, 2002. Film.

Chapter 2
[vi] *Reimagining Church: Pursuing the Dream of Organic Christianity*. Colorado Springs: David C. Cook, 2008.

[vii] Cole, Neil. "The Life Transformation Group System by Neil Cole." CMA Resources. May 19, 2009. Accessed January 5, 2015. https://www.cmaresources.org/article/ltg.
[viii] Anderson, Brian, and Steve Atkerson. *House Church: Simple, Strategic, Scriptural*. Atlanta: New Testament Reformation Fellowship, 2008.
[ix] Fee, Gordon D. *The First Epistle to the Corinthians*. Grand Rapids: W.B. Eerdmans, 1987.
[x] Gooch, John. *Christian History & Biography*. Carol Stream: Christianity Today International, 2004.
[xi] Inspired by Zola Levitt Ministries, a resource for understanding Christianity from a Jewish perspective. http://www.levitt.com/

Chapter 3
[xii] *Right Here, Right Now: Everyday Mission for Everyday People*. Grand Rapids: Baker Books, 2011.
[xiii] *The Help*. New York: Amy Einhorn Books, 2009.; *The Help*. Touchstone Home Entertainment, 2011. Film.

Chapter 4
[xiv] *Grown Ups*. Sony Pictures Home Entertainment, 2010. Film.
[xv] "PW Talks With Francis Chan: Multiplying Disciples." PublishersWeekly.com. October 15, 2012. Accessed January 5, 2015. http://www.publishersweekly.com/pw/by-topic/industry-news/religion/article/54392-pw-talks-with-francis-chan-multiplying-disciples.html.

Chapter 5
[xvi] Bright, Bill. "Your Personal Guide to Fasting and Prayer." Cru.org. Accessed January 5, 2015. http://www.cru.org/train-and-grow/devotional-life/personal-guide-to-fasting.1.html.
[xvii] Wesley, John. *Sermons on Several Occasions*. London: Epworth Press, 1944.
[xviii] Foster, Richard J. *Celebration of Discipline: The Path to Spiritual Growth*. San Francisco: Harper & Row, 1988.

Chapter 6
[xix] **Sparks, Austin T. as quoted in:** Frank Viola. *Reimagining Church: Pursuing the Dream of Organic Christianity.* Colorado Springs: David C. Cook, 2008.
[xx] Gladwell, Malcolm. *The Tipping Point: How Little Things Can Make A Big Difference.* Boston: Little, Brown, 2000.
[xxi] Beare, Sally. *50 Secrets of the World's Longest Living People.* New York: Marlowe & Co., 2006.; *Forks Over Knives.* Monica Beach Media, 2011. Film.

Chapter 7
[xxii] Chan, Francis, and Danae Yankoski. *Forgotten God: Reversing Our Tragic Neglect of the Holy Spirit.* Colorado Springs: David C. Cook, 2009.
[xxiii] Chambers, Oswald. "Spiritual Vision through Personal Character." My Utmost For His Highest. Accessed January 5, 2015. http://utmost.org/spiritual-vision-through-personal-purity-2/.
[xxiv] Micklethwait, John, and Adrian Wooldridge. *God Is Back: How the Global Revival of Faith Is Changing the World.* New York: Penguin Press, 2009.
[xxv] Simson, Wolfgang. *Houses That Change the World: The Return of the House Churches.* Carlisle, Cumbria, U.K.: OM, 2001.; Cole, Neil. *Primal Fire: Reigniting the Church with the Five Gifts of Jesus.* Tyndale Momentum, 2014.
[xxvi] Gladwell, Malcolm. *Outliers: The Story of Success.* Back Bay Books, 2011.

Chapter 8
[xxvii] *The Shawshank Redemption.* Columbia Pictures, 1994. Film.

Chapter 9
[xxviii] "Blight." Merriam-Webster. Accessed January 5, 2015. http://www.merriam-webster.com/dictionary/blight.
[xxix] Bonhoeffer, Dietrich, and Ron Klug. *40-day Journey with Dietrich Bonhoeffer.* Minneapolis: Augsburg Books, 2007.
[xxx] Keller, Timothy J. *The Reason for God: Belief in an Age of Skepticism.* New York: Dutton, 2008.

Chapter 10
[xxxi] Viola, Frank. *From Eternity to Here: Rediscovering the Ageless Purpose of God*. Colorado Springs: David C. Cook, 2009.
[xxxii] Anderson, Brian, and Steve Atkerson. *House Church: Simple, Strategic, Scriptural*. Atlanta: New Testament Reformation Fellowship, 2008.
[xxxiii] Tolkien, J. R. R. *The Two Towers; Being the Second Part of The Lord of the Rings*. Boston: Houghton Mifflin, 1965.

www.ingramcontent.com/pod-product-compliance
Lightning Source LLC
Chambersburg PA
CBHW070107080526
44586CB00013B/1221